GH00372852

PRAISE

YOU HAVE TO SAY
I'M PRETTY,
YOU'RE MY
MOTHER

'With humour and empathy, a mother (Stephanie Pierson) and a psychotherapist (Phyllis Cohen) write forthrightly to mums (and dads) about separation from and connection with adolescent daughters; how to model for and speak with them to preserve and foster their self-esteem.'

– Andrea Marks, M.D., Adolescent Medicine specialist and co-author of *Healthy Teens, Body and Soul: A Parent's Complete Guide to Adolescent Health*

'*You Have to Say I'm Pretty, You're My Mother* offers practical wisdom, clarity, hope, and plain talk to mothers (and fathers) concerned about how to help their daughters develop and sustain a healthy regard for themselves and their bodies. With grace and good humour, Pierson and Cohen show empathy and respect for mothers (and daughters); their appreciation for the complexities of mothering a daughter make this gem of a book particularly useful. I am grateful that it exists, and will recommend it to many a parent.'

– Sheila Reindl, Ed.D., psychologist, Harvard University, and author of *Sensing the Self: Women's Recovery from Bulimia*

'A gifted writer and an insightful psychotherapist examine the developing image of teenage girls. What they capture will resonate with mothers (and daughters) everywhere. Their wise advice benefits us all.'

– Dr. Jana Klauer, Research Fellow, New York Obesity Research Institute, St. Luke's-Roosevelt Hospital

'We all know that girls are sorely troubled by body-related issues, and we may even understand why, but how many of us have a clue about how to handle the problem? What parent hasn't wondered when and how to intervene when a beloved child seems to be recklessly veering towards self-destructive and/or self-sabotaging behaviour. This book fills the void. Keep it under your mattress – I will!'

– Renée Fleming, Mother of two pre-teenage girls, and in her spare time, opera star

'*You Have to Say I'm Pretty, You're My Mother* is an essential book for parents who find themselves struggling with the ubiquitous dilemma of how to help a daughter whose self-esteem is being overly determined by her body-image. The authors guide parents through an invaluable series of practical "do's and don'ts", and emphasize the extreme importance of mothers and fathers looking deep to "get healthy" themselves in regard to body ideals and communication style. I embrace their thesis that a mother must first take care of herself and become the most mindful person she can before she can hope to be an effective role model for her child.'

– Deborah E. Lynn, MD, Consultant Clinical Faculty, University of California, Los Angeles (UCLA), Division of Child and Adolescent Psychiatry

Also by Stephanie Pierson

Because I'm the Mother, That's Why!

Vegetables Rock! A Complete Guide for Teenage Vegetarians

YOU HAVE TO SAY I'M PRETTY, YOU'RE MY MOTHER

How to Help Your Daughter
Learn to Love Her Body and Herself

Stephanie Pierson
and Phyllis Cohen

Vermilion
LONDON

1 3 5 7 9 10 8 6 4 2

Copyright © 2003 by Stephanie Pierson and Phyllis Cohen

Stephanie Pierson and Phyllis Cohen have asserted their right to be identified as the authors of this work in accordance with the Copyright, Designs and Patents Act, 1988.

All rights reserved. No part of this publication may be reproduced, stored in a retrieval system, or transmitted in any form or by any means, electronic, mechanical, photocopying, recording or otherwise, without the prior permission of the copyright owners.

First published in 2003 by Simon & Schuster, Inc.
This edition published in 2003 by Vermilion,
an imprint of Ebury Press, Random House,
20 Vauxhall Bridge Road, London SW1V 2SA
www.randomhouse.co.uk

Random House Australia (Pty) Limited
20 Alfred Street, Milsons Point, Sydney,
New South Wales 2061, Australia

Random House New Zealand Limited
18 Poland Road, Glenfield,
Auckland 10, New Zealand

Random House South Africa (Pty) Limited
Endulini, 5A Jubilee Road,
Parktown 2193, South Africa

The Random House Group Limited Reg. No. 954009

Designed by Bonni Leon

Papers used by Vermilion are natural recyclable products made from wood grown in sustainable forests.

Printed and bound by Mackays of Chatham Plc, Chatham, Kent

A CIP catalogue record for this book
is available from the British Library

ISBN 0-09-188456-X

SP: For Phoebe

PLC: To my mother

ACKNOWLEDGMENTS

Marcy Posner, for literary navigation and nurturing.

Sydny Miner, editor of extraordinary skill and insight.

Tom Connell, for technical brilliance, infinite patience, and knowing that *deleted* just means a little harder to find.

Laura Holmes, thanks for staying on top throughout.

Nancy Inglis, who took our words to heart.

Megan Connell, Katie Hall, Elizabeth Sandberg, Anne Burns, Dorothy Kalins, Dominique Bigar Khan, Miss Lindsay Carleton, Caroline Schaefer, Sheila Reindl, Amy Peck, Kathy Levine, DeEttra Kudera, Alexis Johnson, Harriet Blumencranz, Rosalie McCabe, Nancy Stephens, Dian Ohrnberger, Lee Davis, Eileen Lambert, Kathleen McNamara, Christine Masters, Marylin Silverman, Patti Goberman, Susan Allport.

PLC: *Thanks for their invaluable contributions:* Robin Brancato, Dr. Arlene Stang, Dr. Janet Geller, Dr. Martha Bragin, Jennifer Hall, CSW, Dr. Leona Jaglom, Marilyn Steisel, CSW, Dr. Martha Black, Lenore Weinstein, Monica Pierrepoint, CSW, Diane Malek, LCSW. Paula Steisel, who helped with research. And my patients, who through their own work become my best teachers.

CONTENTS

Introduction   1

CHAPTER 1
Body Image Basics   10

CHAPTER 2
The Battles of Body Ownership:
She's *Your* Daughter, but It's *Her* Body   21

CHAPTER 3
Your Relationship Is a Process   27

CHAPTER 4
Take a Good Look at Yourself   51

CHAPTER 5
"You Have to Say I'm Pretty, You're My Mother"   69

CHAPTER 6
What Kind of Mother Are You?   92

CHAPTER 7
Husbands and Fathers   104

CHAPTER 8
Teenage Girls, the Care and Feeding Of   130

CHAPTER 9
Sex   162

Contents

CHAPTER 10
When to Worry, When to Intervene, How to Help   181

CHAPTER 11
What Our Daughters Are Saying About Us   215

Resources   231
P.S.   237
Index   239

YOU HAVE TO SAY
I'M PRETTY,
YOU'RE MY
MOTHER

INTRODUCTION

THIS BOOK STARTED five years ago when my then fourteen-year-old daughter, Phoebe, was alternately throwing up in her school bathroom and starving herself at home. Somehow, at what seemed like warp speed, Phoebe went from being happy to being miserable. From not worrying about her weight to insisting on having *two* scales in her bathroom and memorizing the calorie count of every morsel of food. From not worrying about how she looked to freezing like a deer in the headlights in front of the nearest mirror and asking, "Do I look particularly fat today?" Day after day after day.

We took Phoebe to a therapist who suggested she draw pictures of rainbows. I went to a therapist who said, "She's such a beautiful girl. How can she have an eating disorder?" My husband and I talked to a psychopharmacologist who said it was probably all biochemical. "Oh, she's just having a hard time adjusting to a new town . . . to a new school . . . to adolescence . . . to two parents who are never home," said her school guidance counselor, hastily adding, "but two parents who love her *very* much."

Phoebe went to an eating disorder clinic where they gave her a healthful diet and told her all about the food pyramid.

"Complex people have complex problems," suggested her pediatrician. "Just look at all the depression that runs in our family," my sister-in-law theorized. "It's all those Sylvia Plath books and Anne Sexton poems she's wallowing in," warned her teacher. And this dubiously positive pronouncement was offered by my mother: "Well, she certainly eats a lot for a girl with anorexia."

Phoebe was in crisis. I was in crisis. Our family was in crisis. And while her eating disorders slowly got better (with time, with family therapy, with counseling, with revelations), her body image issues remained. Phoebe, always precocious, might have been first on her block to obsess about her looks, but soon most of her friends had their own problems, too. And I gradually realized that most of America is caught up with body image issues. There's an absolute epidemic today of beautiful, accomplished adolescent girls who are convinced that they're fat and ugly, who believe that looks are everything and that *their* looks don't measure up to some impossible ideal. They are matched by loving and well-meaning mothers who feel blindsided, helpless, clueless, terrified, and guilty (sometimes all at once) and who invariably have their own unresolved body image issues.

Always a problem solver (instant when possible), when the problems became overwhelming, I read everything. I talked to every smart person I could find. I got conflicting opinions, outdated information, misinformation, suggestions that might have been helpful if Phoebe were ten. I read books written in some sort of academic shrink-y language I couldn't understand, breezy magazine articles that both minimized and oversimplified complex subjects, overwrought books with only worst-case scenarios. I saw TV shows on body image topics that sensationalized *everything*. I found bits and pieces of what sounded like good advice on the Internet but didn't know how reliable the sources were.

Oddly enough, it was when I read Mary Pipher's brilliantly insightful *Reviving Ophelia* that I felt the most helpless. While this was the one book that helped me get an overview and explained the magnitude of the problem, after I finished it, I still didn't have a clue about what to do with Phoebe. How was I to respond to her saying, "Will you look at how gross my stomach is?" when her stomach was as flat as a washboard? How was I to answer "What's wrong with my knees?" when there was nothing wrong with her knees? And when no matter *what* I said, she came back with, "Well, you *have* to say that, you're my mother."

Where was the book to help mothers like me who need to *address* body image problems, not just understand them? Where could mothers go for practical advice and straightforward strategies? Where could mothers get answers to the universal mother questions: "But what do I do now?" "What do I say to her?" "How do I get through to her?"

With all due modesty, I have to say there is no one less qualified on her own to write a body image book than I am. What I do have is a lot more painful experience than I would like to. And the right questions. Lots of them. Why does a beautiful, seemingly happy young girl feel so unbeautiful?

Why does my daughter hate her body? Why is she so preoccupied with it? Why does she seem to hate *parts* of her body ("I hate my feet," "I hate my hips," "I hate my butt")? Why does she think she's fat when she wears a size two? Why is her self-esteem based on the circumference of her thighs? If she's smart enough to learn AP Physics and Honors Calculus, why can't she learn to love herself? Are we too close or not close enough? How do I know? Am I too concerned? And if *I'm* feeling this helpless and powerless, how can I get help from a husband who seems helpless, powerless, and clueless? Are other girls suffering the way my daughter is? Is every other mother sleeping soundly at night?

How can I help my daughter when I don't understand her and she won't talk to me? Why doesn't she take my advice? Is it a phase? Will she outgrow it? What does it mean? Who can I blame for her problems? Barbie, Kate Moss, Jenny Craig, the cute varsity football captain she's got a crush on, myself? Is it a question of blame at all? Do I even have the power to make my daughter's problems better or worse?

After I had all the right questions, I looked for someone with answers. Through some karmic miracle (maybe I had suffered enough in this lifetime) I found Phyllis Cohen, a New York psychotherapist specializing in adolescents, who after thirty years of practice, of teaching and writing and lecturing and listening, knows how serious and pervasive body image issues are. Phyllis's practice often includes mothers as well as adolescents, so she understands these issues from both vantage points. She knows that what is crucial to achieving success is the ongoing emotional education of both mothers and daughters. And no one is a better teacher than Phyllis.

Our shared goal was to write a book of fundamental lessons and advice, a book so practical, it wouldn't just be read, it would be *used*—as a guide, a compass, and a road map. We two speak with one voice for mothers of daughters from thirteen to nineteen, to help you help *your* daughter with the staggering number of body image issues that come up on her radar screen from the moment she wakes up in the morning to the time she goes to bed at night. From looks to weight to glossy retouched magazine perfection to cosmetic surgery to disordered eating to eating disorders to mothers on diets to health clubs to makeup to depression to cutting to suicide to cyber relationships to sex to bare midriffs to bikinis to body piercing to MTV to numbers on the scale to SAT scores.

When we told people we were writing a book about body image issues, they frequently responded, "Oh, a book about eating disorders." Body image issues seem to have become synonymous with anorexia, bulimia, bingeing, starving, overeating, obesity—the highly visible area of eating disorders. But body image is a much broader idea. It is linked to self-image, self-esteem, and self-confidence. It is the sense you have of yourself as a person. And once you see that body image is a much larger issue, you can begin to understand it in a larger and more accurate context.

The first question to be answered in this book is why so many body image problems exist in the first place. Many mothers correctly perceive that the passage from childhood to adulthood is a lot more complex for their daughters than it was for them. The pressure on adolescent girls is more intense; their choices are less clear; their reactions are more extreme. Today getting from twelve to twenty in one sane, self-confident piece is a challenge up there with scaling Mount Everest. The real difficulty lies in the fact that the teenage years are when these girls are defining themselves as individuals. These days most of that definition begins, and sometimes ends, with how they look. Who they are feels more about what's outside and less about what's inside, because they invest so much of their sense of self in their bodies.

So real problems exist; you're not imagining them. The next question is, how is your daughter likely to deal with these problems? She'll express her unhappiness through something that has to do with her body. Or (does this sound familiar?) she'll take it out on you.

So here the two of you are, often at loggerheads—sometimes friendly and comfortable with each other, but more often skirmishing. You know how important it is to have a relationship with your daughter; the problem is, you just can't figure out how to *relate*. You want to talk to her about her school, her life, her friends, and her feelings. But if she wants to talk to you at all, she wants to talk about her hips (too big), her hair (too wavy), her thighs (too fat), her eyes (too whatever). Somehow all you have in common is the fact that you can't talk to each other. And if you ever swore to yourself that you would never behave toward your daughter the way your mother behaved toward you, this is probably the point where you find yourself doing exactly that. And with no more success than your mother had.

A first piece of advice: Do not despair. Do not give up. Do not think it's too late to make it better or do it differently. Know that in the course of helping your daughter develop a healthy body image, you will experience as many highs as lows, as much laughter as tears. Have faith that you and your daughter *can* have a mutually satisfying relationship and that you can effect positive changes. Why? Because you and your daughter love each other. You need each other and you both need a relationship that works. It may feel as though the girl you once loved is gone, along with all the familiar ties that connected the two of you, but be reassured. The mother-daughter bond that was formed when your daughter was an infant is still strong. No matter how deeply it may be buried under all the conflicts that have grown between you, the connection is still there and always will be, and you can find it when you start to look for it. Once you recover that bond, you will be able to do two vital things: start listening to your daughter and start learning from her. At the same time, this connection will help your daughter start to learn more about you as a person and to listen to what *you* have to say. This genuine mutual communication is the basis for a loving, supportive relationship.

To even begin to take a first positive step, you need to stop feeling guilty about everything. Stop blaming either your daughter or yourself for every argument that results from your daughter's hating her body, from your saying something critical to her, from her saying something mean to you. And no matter how many times she tells you that you don't do anything right, no matter how mean-spirited or verbally abusive she is, do not come away concluding, "She's right, I can't do or say anything right. She's impossible to understand. She hates me. I give up." You are doing lots of things right, and you'll do more. So don't devalue yourself.

For your daughter, it's all about testing. She's testing limits, she's testing reality, she's testing your love, she's testing your acceptance or rejection of who she is, and she's testing body boundaries. While she's being hysterical, hateful, and horrible, you need to be firm. As the grown-up in the relationship, it's your job to set boundaries. While you're setting limits about her body, remember that it's her body, not yours. If she's doing something risky (like having promiscuous sex, abusing drugs, bingeing and purging, or yo-yo dieting), then you must intervene. Otherwise, respect her boundaries.

To help make all of this less abstract, throughout the book we'll give you what you need: steps, strategies, suggestions, and templates.

Basically, your job is to figure out what isn't working and why, to find ways to better understand and connect with your daughter. Ours is to give you the tools to do this. If we do our job and you do yours, we'll reach our shared goal: your daughter will have a positive body image. You'll have your life back.

Two disclaimers: Phoebe (inspiration and intelligent

reader) points out that, in her opinion, this book occasionally reads like one of those public television nature shows, where the announcer intones, "The young female is apt to be skittish, if not dangerous. She stays close to her pack and resists any attempt to lure her out of the bush." We ask any girl who reads the book to understand that we don't mean to talk about her as if she were a young gazelle or zebra.

The other disclaimer is that Phoebe (expert critic and stickler for accuracy) also points out that although we're not adolescent girls ourselves, we presume to speak for them and to know everything they're thinking and saying. We feel strongly that we have captured both the spirit and the essence of these girls without misrepresenting them, but the nature of a book like this is to universalize, generalize, and make some assumptions. We do presume smart readers. If you and your daughter (and Phoebe) don't take it totally literally, this book will make more sense.

Chapter 1

BODY IMAGE BASICS

THERE ARE A FEW CORE QUESTIONS all mothers have: Why is my daughter so focused on her body? Why does she have such a negative body image? Do all girls have body image issues? Which girls are most vulnerable? Is my daughter one of them?

There are three core facts that are at the heart of all these questions. First, there are more factors than ever before (cultural, relational, sexual, social) that contribute to your daughter's having problems loving the way she looks.

Second, while there are many factors in your relationship with your daughter that will influence her behavior, how you see your *own* body (and communicate that) is the biggest influence on how your daughter sees hers.

Third, your relationship with your daughter is part of an ongoing process. In spite of all the discouraging and difficult things that may happen between you, time is on your side. You will find many ways over the next few years to help your daughter see her body and herself in a positive light.

. . .

FOR MANY REASONS, your daughter's focus on her body is only natural. Teenagers who are starting to separate from their mothers and fathers need to consolidate that separation by taking full ownership of their bodies. This long process—a girl's gradual separation and her growing autonomy—starts as early as ten or eleven and goes all the way to late adolescence, from seventeen to nineteen. What does this mean? Well, from our experience it means that during these years she will spend half her time looking in a mirror and the other half fighting with her mother about some aspect of her looks—whether her skirt is too tight, whether her eye shadow is too bright, whether piercing her navel is a constitutional right. Most mother-daughter skirmishes are about control issues. Most of these control issues are about separation. And the battleground where they are all waged is the body. The question "Whose body is it, anyway?" comes up over and over in different ways.

The more you understand these issues and what your daughter is going through, the easier it will be for you to protect her from potential problems, to solve existing ones, and to exert a strong positive influence on what is an inherently bumpy passage. *Easier,* by the way, is a relative term. You may find that you feel paralyzed by your fears of a passage that you don't really understand and by a daughter you understand less and less. You may feel anxious and worried just knowing you're being pushed away by your daughter. You may react to her crushing contempt by feeling both angry and scared that she'll move even farther away from you. Or you may believe that her disdain and her anger are so fixed that you can't do anything to change them.

But while her attitude may go (in a matter of minutes) from the hysterical to the hostile, and while her "Leave me alone!" or "Get out of my life" statements aren't exactly conducive to a heart-to-heart talk, you can't give up or bail out. Mothers matter more than anyone else to an adolescent girl, and everything you are both going through is part of a process your daughter *needs* to go through to figure out who she is as a separate and unique person. This ongoing struggle is crucial both in contributing to and in resolving body image issues. Remember when you thought giving birth to her was hard?

There are understandable reasons behind your daughter's struggles. From her point of view, the mother she once knew is now someone who seems to understand her less and wants to control her more, so instead of loving you blindly and unconditionally as she did when she was younger, she now sees her relationship with you as ambivalent, combative, and puzzling. For her to successfully separate and gain autonomy, she needs to take some of the luster off the idealized image she has of you and replace it by criticism that often borders on contempt. From a mother's perspective, the child you once knew has morphed into another being whose behavior is mystifying and often disturbing. As far as you're concerned, this would be the part in the movie where someone from outer space has replaced the adorable, loving child with an evil alien adolescent twin.

It may be a small comfort, but in these moments and

moods your daughter, the teenage alien, feels every bit as alienated from herself as she does from you. Remember your own adolescence? You know from your own experience how hard it is to reconcile the person you are with the person you really wanted to be—how hard it was when you realized that your breast size was never going to be perfect or that your hair would never be shinier than it was. Adolescence is when our dreams and fantasies of "When I grow up, I'm going to be . . ." come into sharp focus. For your daughter, it's the first time that these girlhood dreams are hitting smack into reality.

This is when she suddenly realizes that she's not the best dancer or the star soccer player. She envies other girls who seem to have it easier or starts comparing herself (unfavorably, of course) with models, athletes, rock stars, and movie stars. The frustrations that stem from her disappointments cause her to devalue who she is. She's suffering from a very real sense of loss; it's painful for her to give up childhood dreams. It's especially painful for her to have to give up the idealized way she saw *you* when she was little. All those images of perfection that once seemed possible now stand in stark contrast to her new, distinctly imperfect, reality. Her face has zits. Her mother has flaws. Her life isn't going to be made into a movie starring Beautiful, Perfect Her!

The result is lots of anger that she directs against herself and sometimes you. Her body is the place these feelings settle, so she takes things out on her body. Her revenge might be something as mild as cutting gym to something extreme, like starving herself.

She critically examines every part of her body: "I hate my butt." "My legs are gross." "If only I had less flabby arms." Every day the mirror brings new disappointments and frustrations. And out of her obsession with what's outside comes her new internalized beliefs: "I hate my body" and "I hate the mother who gave me this body."

Suddenly the expression "painfully aware" makes perfect sense. Your daughter is painfully aware of who she *isn't*, and she hasn't yet figured out who she *is*. So she needs to explore, experiment, fail, and succeed by trying on many different personas. ("I'm a Goth," "I'm a hippie," "I'm into boys . . . body piercing . . . Buddha . . .") What's important is that you see this role playing for what it is and that you don't panic. Now is the time to pick your battles wisely. Is she making a harmless statement about her autonomy or is she doing something that could be harmful? By not saying no to everything, by not overreacting, by being the grown-up in the relationship, you'll be able to help your daughter get through this experimentation. You'll help her understand it and you'll be there to cushion any crash landings, help her right herself, and help her learn from her failures.

While she's trying out different roles and hair colors (usually the ones that don't wash out), your daughter also feels compelled to find some way to defend herself against her pain, her losses, her uncertainty. Her answer is not to find other things to focus on, but to concentrate even more on her body and to think in a new (and decidedly distorted) way about it. She is more proactive (good news) and less rational (bad news). She now believes that if she can just fix what's on the outside, she'll feel better about what's on the inside. Every mother knows this adolescent logic: "If I dye my hair pink, I'll be a knockout." "If I can look like the girl in the MTV video, then I'll be happy." "If I shave all the hair on my body and put on self-tanner, then I'll look so cool."

It's almost impossible for your daughter to understand that part of the process of becoming her own person is finding a place for her childhood dreams and wishes and knowing that they don't have to be lost forever. This is a very important part of your input as a mother. You can help by keeping her grounded in reality—reminding her of what her *real* assets, skills, and strengths are. Your consistent reinforcement is like the lifeline in a tempest. She may whirl furiously around, saying, "You don't know what you're talking about," but your stability and positive, consistent validation of her will prove the most valuable asset in helping her separate and gain a positive self-image.

Every small, calm, rational gesture you make toward her is helping her achieve her larger long-term goals: to aspire to more realistic dreams, to gradually integrate all of her experiences, to successfully cope with her new reality, and in time, to attain a well-rounded sense of herself.

Your job, as always, is to keep a grip on reality and not feel decimated by her fitful progress, her distorted thinking, her inability to really hear what you're saying to her. Even if you have the patience of a saint, it's hard to hang in there through your daughter's inscrutability or toxic anger, her hostility, her deeply hurtful personal attacks. It helps to know that as profoundly painful as it is for you, your daughter would have a hard time growing and maturing without expressing some of these feelings. If you think *your* job is hard, your daughter's is even harder. In order to grow up, she has to do two contradictory things—separate from the mother with whom she has had a lifelong bond and continue to identify with her—both at the same time.

That is the job description of adolescence for mothers and daughters: A girl has to separate from her mother and develop a sense of who she is as she goes from being a child to becoming a woman. And her mother has to help provide her with the tools and guidance she needs to separate and to develop a healthy sense of herself that's more than skin deep.

Why is it harder for some girls than others? Are some girls more in danger of developing a negative body image and the problems that go with it? The answer is yes. There are some real, quantifiable factors that put girls at risk. The most vulnerable girls are:

- A girl who, growing up, is either significantly underweight or overweight; one whose mother has attached great anxiety to this and made it clear that it is a problem.
- A girl whose mother is preoccupied with her own weight, looks, and social success, and who projects these worries onto her daughter.
- A girl who has had problems with social skills, shyness, or overattachment to her mother.
- A girl whose father is critical of her and her appearance.

This kind of father, threatened by his daughter's budding sexuality, may tease his daughter or find subtle ways to put down her developing body.

The more risk factors there are, the more chance there is that a body image problem will develop. And while the mantra today is, "Well, it must be the influence of MTV/a fashion magazine/the music," it's just not that simple. Media assaults and the lack of the consistent presence of a parent to help filter and moderate what a child is seeing are a potent combination. The bottom line is, a girl needs a loving, devoted, vigilant parent who can help her see through this distorted worldview and decode it.

If you know that your daughter is at risk, is there a way to anticipate problems? Yes. Once risk factors have been identified, you can be alert to signs and signals from your daughter that body image problems may be taking hold. Look for signs of depression, eating changes, isolation, extreme mood swings, loss of energy, loss of friends—anything that signals that she's not herself.

At the same time you can look for opportunities to fight back—to say or do things that are smart and supportive and helpful. How to help:

Provide a reality check. Very often girls who have a negative body image are negative about *everything*—the whole world is sour. Help your daughter see that not everything is so bad. Be prepared: when you offer help, she'll probably be negative about that, too. As perverse as it may sound, don't be critical of her negativity; go with it and you'll get better results. For example, it actually helps to start off with something that sounds negative, like, "You may not find this helpful *but* . . ." Then say something supportive, such as, "If you'd like to get out and go to a friend's house, I'll give you a ride." The objective is to at least get her out of her room, where she is feeling isolated and miserable. Alternatively, agree to help her get whatever she is convinced will turn her life around (a new outfit, cool shoes, a totally different haircut, glitter makeup). Don't expect an instant attitude change and keep trying.

❧

Don't be the kind of mother who feels upbeat about everything, the one whose enthusiasm feels inappropriate and false, who says to her gloomy daughter, "What a beautiful day! Why don't you go have a fun bike ride?" If you want to be cheerfully manic, be cheerfully manic on your own. And don't put your daughter down, telling her, "You have no right to be so depressed. It's a beautiful day. Snap out of it." Your daughter doesn't need a controlling mother trying to micromanage her every mood.

❧

Don't be the kind of mother who has an answer for everything. If your daughter looks in the mirror a million times a day, don't say a word. It's maddening. But it's normal.

❧

So is talking on the telephone about nothing for hours on end. Don't listen. Don't hover in the doorway of her room, looking for a good opening to have a "meaningful conversation." If you're going to stand by her door, quickly say whatever word of encouragement you want, then leave.

❧

Do encourage her to form relationships with positive female role models. Osmosis does work.

WHAT EVERY MOTHER NEEDS TO KNOW

Fat is a code word for an emotion, not a number on the scale. Fat is also the vocabulary for your daughter's emotions; it may be the only way she knows how to talk about what's bothering her.

Listen to what your daughter says, but don't take what she says about her body literally. If she says, "I'm so fat," don't say, "Well, just go on a diet and lose five pounds." She's not talking about dieting; she's talking about her feelings.

Remember that she's growing into her body and it's not always a great fit. You're used to your body. She's not used to hers.

There are all sorts of fears and insecurities your daughter may have about herself and her body. Don't dismiss these; they are the best clues you'll get about her inner thoughts.

Your daughter is bombarded by girl talk about bodies all day long, and she believes her friends more than you. This is normal. Help her think things through.

Be aware of what you're adding to the mix: how you talk about *your* body, *your* weight, *your* appearance. Think about what kind of role model *you* are.

If your daughter really does have a weight problem, she has to be the one who decides how she wants to handle it. Or *if* she wants to handle it. Of course, if her weight is creating a serious health problem, you need to construct a plan that addresses your daughter's physical and emotional well-being, one that can help her lose weight and gain self-esteem.

Chapter 2

THE BATTLES OF BODY OWNERSHIP:
SHE'S *YOUR* DAUGHTER, BUT IT'S *HER* BODY

YOU DON'T LIKE the Gap tiny tank tops she wears or that strand of hair that's always falling in her eyes? You *know* she'd look better if she lost five pounds or if she'd just firm up those jiggly thighs? Guess what. She's *your* daughter, but it's *her* body. And while the question "Whose body is it, anyway?" might sound like a quiz show title, starting about when your daughter is twelve, it's going to be both the central question and a major source of conflict between you—not just for a few months, but for a few years. A few *long* years. How you handle it can make the difference between having a daughter who, despite any problems she may have, is at ease with herself and a daughter who takes all her problems, focuses them on her body, then feels terrible every time she looks in the mirror.

The first battles around body ownership begin in early adolescence with the onset of puberty. This is when an adolescent girl needs to consolidate her separation from her mother by slowly gaining full ownership of her body. To acknowledge this gain and to assert her independence, she needs to push her mother away, and one of the ways she pushes first and hardest is around body issues. The opening volley is some declaration on her part that "I'm not a kid anymore." Which would be fine except that she sure looks like a little girl to you, especially considering that you still need to remind her to brush her teeth and not to wear her flip-flops in the snow. This stage is almost a reprise of the "You are not the boss of me" phase she went through when she was two. "You can't tell me what to wear," she proclaims. "You can't make me wear these stupid barrettes." "You can't tell me what looks good. Look at what *you're* wearing." This is when even the gentlest suggestion reduces her to tears, when unhappiness turns into instant hysteria, and when even the kindest remark is misconstrued as the vilest criticism. With the slam of the bathroom door, the war of body ownership has officially begun. "I don't know," her dazed parents say. "It's like she went to sleep one night a sweet little girl and woke up a monster." A highly developed monster with a kind of scary (to her and to you) new sexuality. Your baby, who can now (even more scary) have a baby of her own.

For the first time since she was a toddler, body boundary issues come up. Back then she learned from you how and when to use the toilet, who could and who couldn't touch her body, what she could do in public and what she should do in private. And now it starts all over again. Will your daughter be willing to talk to you about what's happening to her body and how she feels about it? If, when she was little, both of you were comfortable expressing your feelings and you had a good physical relationship, you'll probably have an easier time of it when she's an adolescent. But even a close earlier relationship isn't a guarantee. You may find that, in spite of your having said and done all the right things, huge barriers go up. These barriers may have more to do with her than with you; some girls have a tough time with the physical changes they're experiencing.

As a rule of thumb, every girl has *some* issues around her changing body. (The book for both of you to read is *The What's Happening to My Body? Book for Girls*, by Lynda Madaras.) The onset of menstruation, in particular, is a very important time in the emotional life of a young girl. For all girls there's some adjustment to be made to the idea of *having* periods, not just because of the bleeding but because of all the newly uncomfortable feelings that seem to spring up from nowhere and appear every month—PMS, bloating, cramps, headaches, food cravings, mood swings.

Some girls have a particularly hard time: A girl whose first menstruation is delayed (some girls don't start until fifteen or sixteen) will feel anxious, worried that she's "not normal." The girl who gets her period before anyone else feels alone and scared. A girl who is overwhelmed by all the changes feels an urgent need for privacy.

Aside from menstruation, there are lots of other body changes that make these girls feel out of control: they're getting zits, they're taller than all the boys in their class, their breasts are huge (at least *they* think so). And where do they take all their rising tension and resentment? Surprise! They not only take it *to* their mother, they often take it *out on* her. They complain, they're cranky, they're impossible to live with.

The tension a girl experiences with her mother sometimes takes the form of a push-pull struggle. She pushes her mother away and then quickly pulls her closer. She loves her mother one minute and dismisses her the next. She's still so immature and inexperienced that she doesn't know what she wants or who she is most of the time. She wants to be comforted, but nothing comforts her. She wants to make it better, but she can't. So she wants her mother to make it better like she always used to. But wait a minute. If her mother babies her, that means she'll be treated like a little girl. And she isn't a little girl anymore, is she?

So the tension mounts and a war inevitably ensues, because getting close to you by fighting with you is the way she can deal with it. She can complain loudly about your bossing her around, she can push you away, and she can be intensely involved with you—all at the same time. Know that for your daughter *any* active engagement or interaction with the enemy is better than none. When your daughter is this confused about your role in her life—friend or foe—she *needs* this war in order to start to separate.

What's the battlefield for this war? Usually the body, and so the struggles are supremely visible. Tattoos, diets, fat phobias, dressing provocatively—the war is all focused on looks, because that's all your daughter sees. And no wonder. The body is primal, it's central; a girl comes from her mother's body, she was nurtured by her mother's body, she probably looks something like her mother, and will, in many ways, turn out like her. So a teenage girl, just by shaving her head, will accomplish a number of goals: she'll push her mother away, she'll have made a creative decision, she'll give her own body uniqueness, and she'll make a statement that she is different. Mostly she will feel in control, temporarily, in her attempt to counter her real feelings of being out of control. She will be saying, in effect, "This is my body, not yours. I'm growing up and I am a sexual being, like it or not. And I'm not a little girl. Except when I feel like it, of course."

Since you can't give her to a convent in Spain until she's twenty-one, how can you coexist in a house that feels like a war zone and in a situation that feels totally no-win, no matter what you do? It's very important that you (a) understand how upsetting it is for your daughter to feel this out of control and (b) introduce the concept of normalcy to her so that she has some small sense of perspective about her body.

Try to talk her through everything. Tune into her body changes and moods. Be sensitive to how she feels about things. Listen to how she reacts and answers. Respond by giving her your feedback and sharing your own experience. If possible, give her the history of the women in your family and share any generational experiences or problems.

Understanding how her body works, knowing that every woman's body responds differently, and realizing that one size doesn't fit all can help a girl. Understanding how her body works can help her accept and adjust to PMS, sore breasts, mood swings, cramps, bloating, food cravings, and normal water weight gain. Many girls compare themselves with their friends, and if a girl has difficult periods she may feel victimized by her body and resentful of her changes. Just helping her define what's normal and what's not is reassuring, and as crazy as this may sound, it's a way of joining and bonding, of bringing your daughter into the family of women.

Understandably, this is a shy time; your daughter may not want to talk as much as you might want her to. Because she's experiencing so many changes all at once, she's easily overwhelmed. Your strong presence and quiet reassurance can go a long way toward providing her with the kind of comfort and empathy that will be helpful to her. But what if she really refuses to talk? What if she won't listen at all? Many girls protect themselves from feeling vulnerable by telling you that they know all there is to know and they don't need your involvement. (For more help on how to communicate, read chapter 3 about process.)

No matter what, except for authorized snooping, respect your daughter's privacy and her modesty. If you don't, she's likely to feel humiliated. Worse yet, you've missed your chance to educate her and help her. Don't violate a confidence. Never say anything private in front of your husband. Don't "share" with a loving grandma or a concerned aunt. The words "Oh, it doesn't matter, it's just your aunt Valerie. We're all girls!" must never come out of your mouth.

Chapter 3

YOUR RELATIONSHIP IS A PROCESS

GOOD PARENTING is more than a series of random attempts at understanding and loving your daughter. It is the ongoing process of staying engaged with her throughout her adolescence. It's learning how to listen to her, how to have a meaningful dialogue, how to keep talking, how to advise her, how to set limits, and how to do all this in a positive way. At its most basic, this process calls for only two things: an emotional tie and an intellectual tie between you and your daughter.

And lest that sound a bit too abstract, be reassured that it comes with this very real promise: if you can stay connected to your daughter in both these ways, you'll slowly gain the coping skills you need to work through problems and crises. You'll be able to withstand the tantrums and tears that accompany these situations by coming to understand that there will be short-term losses and ultimately long-term gains. You'll know that a door she slams one day can be reopened the next. And bit by bit you'll get a much-needed perspective on a passage that is neither quick nor smooth.

The process of successful mothering in adolescence requires you to see beyond a girl who is uncharacteristically moody, unpredictable, irrational, and most strikingly, unresponsive to you. It requires you to make an effort to find the things you can still love about her. (This can be surprisingly difficult; many mothers find their teenage daughters most lovable when the girls are asleep.) It doesn't mean blanket acceptance of what your daughter may be doing or saying or the way she's acting, but it means seeing beyond her behavior to the person within. There's an important difference between "I don't love your pierced tongue, your black lipstick, your smart-ass attitude, your constant criticism" and "I do love *you.*"

When she says something insulting to you, like, "You're so fat and out of shape, you wouldn't have a clue whether *I'm* too skinny," or, "It's been so long since *you've* had sex, no wonder you're so obsessed with *my* sex life," you need to make it instantly clear to her that her behavior is both inappropriate and unacceptable. Your response needs to be calm, simple, and unequivocal: "Whatever it is you want me to know, that's okay. Whatever you think of me is okay. But you can't speak to me that way. I respect you. You need to respect me."

Why does she think she can say outrageous things like this? Hard as it is to believe and painful as it is to accept, sometimes your daughter doesn't really believe you're a human being with feelings. Or if she does, she thinks you're a human being she doesn't want to be around and you would make her life simpler by just going away. Saying and doing hurtful things to you is the best way she can think of to distance herself and prove to you that she's not your little girl. So don't expect her to show you any mercy. She can be so totally self-absorbed that she may be shocked at how hurt you are, how withdrawn you've become. She won't understand for the life of her why two hours after a big argument, you're not dying to take her to the mall to go shopping. How sensitive and overreactive you've become in your old age, she thinks. Obviously *you've* got a big problem.

So forget any help from her. And don't waste your time reminding her that you carried her in your womb for nine long months, had morning sickness practically the whole time, and didn't sleep soundly for the whole first year because she was the most colicky baby ever. Staying connected is up to you. *You're* the one who needs to hang in there. Begin by *finding* that positive connection. Remind yourself that no one in the world knows your daughter better than you do. After all, your love for her is rooted in the earliest, most powerful attachment that human beings make. And even though you often feel as if you're on two different planets, this attachment forms a mother-daughter bond that's like an unbreakable thread; you can pick it up at any time and find that the love between you is alive and intact.

It's this essential bond that allows you to have empathy with your daughter as she struggles to grow into womanhood. When you express this empathy, she is able to listen to you, value what you have to say, and identify with you. You have succeeded in engaging her in a process that will lead to a relationship that works.

An example: Your daughter is in tears. She's getting ready to go to a party and her face has just broken out. She's too embarrassed to tell you how big a deal it really is and that there's going to be a boy there she's got a crush on. You know from your own experience that no amount of false reassurance, no breezy "It's not the end of the world" casualness, will comfort her. Remember your own adolescence, when zits only seemed to come out in full force when they knew you needed to look fabulous.

What you need here is empathy. First, if she'll let you, give her a reassuring hug. You could say something like, "I know how terrible this is. It used to happen to me all the time." Then, respecting her boundaries, offer to help. "So let's see what we can do. Let's get out all the makeup and concealer and zit stuff and we'll do the best we can." Be generous with your time and your support and, if it feels right, any humiliating stories from your own adolescence. See if you can both laugh about something, which will help your daughter take a few steps back from the emotional edge she was about to go over fifteen minutes ago.

With empathy it's possible for you to tell your daughter what you appreciate and admire about her in a way that she can understand and take in. She can feel good about herself and even, for a fleeting moment, good about you. Without it, nothing works.

Here's an example of what *doesn't* work:

NICOLE *(upset because her best friend is going out with a new guy, leaving her to sit home alone on Saturday night):* I can't believe Lizzie ditched me. So now I have to stay home. Alone.

MOTHER: Just because Lizzie is going out with Scott doesn't mean you can't go to the party. And I don't understand how Lizzie ever got Scott. You're so much prettier than she is. And being thin like Lizzie isn't everything.

NICOLE *(can't even deal with the fat comment):* You don't know anything about me! And you think this frizzy, freaky hair is pretty?

MOTHER: There's nothing wrong with your hair.

NICOLE *(frustrated, defensive, and ready to blame her mother for everything): You're* the one who won't let me straighten it and dye it blond. Maybe then someone would ask me out.

MOTHER *(ultimate lack of empathy):* You have no one to blame but yourself. You could go to that party. But maybe you'd rather stay home and feel sorry for yourself.

NICOLE: I hate you. Get out of my life. *(slams door; calls up Lizzie to complain about mother; doesn't say civil word to mother for a week)*

Girls this age spend a lot of energy provoking their mothers, attacking them, and then pushing them away. And they're very good at it. It's their seemingly heartless, completely maddening, and often brilliantly successful way of trying to separate. But if you can see their behavior for what it is—more knee-jerk reaction than premeditated matricide—you'll be more likely to find a way of empathizing with your daughter. So of all the things you hope your daughter is successful at, hope she *isn't* successful at pushing you away. Because the fact is, the girls who succeed are the girls in greatest peril.

What if your daughter is so impossible that she *has* succeeded in pushing you away? This is the point where you need to look at yourself. It is possible that you're contributing to the problem. Once you've been pushed to the limit, it's easy to lose your patience. You don't always feel like being your daughter's own personal cheerleader. It's easy to be judgmental, critical, offended, snappish, unsupportive, frustrated, sarcastic, and bitchy. It's hard to always be the grown-up. So when you find yourself saying or doing things that only make the situation worse, know that this happens to every mother. Step back, remind yourself that you are indeed the parent, then reconnect any way that seems even remotely possible and right for you.

JODY *(accusing):* I can't find my Walkman. Where did you put it? Why are you always moving my stuff?

MOTHER *(neutral; testing waters; trying to break the ice after a fight):* Daddy tripped on it, so I moved it. The last time I saw it, it was on your desk.

JODY *(with attitude):* I looked there and I didn't see it. You probably threw it out.

MOTHER *(trying to lighten it up):* If I was going to start throwing stuff out, I'd begin with every pair of old sneakers that you can't bear to throw out—all twenty pairs since nursery school.

JODY *(faintly smiling; faintly sarcastic): Very* funny. Maybe I should throw out your old flannel bathrobe, or your million-year-old college sweatshirt.

MOTHER *(trying to keep it light and funny):* Hey, that hurt! That sweatshirt is priceless.

JODY: You mean because it's an antique?

You know how when you start to learn tennis, you're happy if you just get a rally going? Talking with your teenage daughter works on the same principle. This might not be a brilliant dialogue, but it is a successful repartee; it keeps a connection going and even has some humor. If your daughter can key in to an old joke or a shared family moment, the situation may be defused. And it's easier for her if you put the joke more on yourself than on her.

Just trying counts.

KATE *(excited):* Mom, aren't these jeans great? They're Caitlin's. She lent them to me.

MOTHER: Blue is such a good choice for you.

KATE *(testing to make sure her mother is really giving her a compliment):* They're not blue, they're green. And it's not the color. They're really cut low. See, they only come up to here.

MOTHER *(seeing lots of skin; at a loss for words):* Well, they look good.

KATE *(dismissive):* You're just saying that. You're not even looking at me.

MOTHER: I *am* looking at you. It's a good cut. And I like the color. They work so well with your eyes; you're lucky that you got Daddy's eyes.

KATE *(sarcastically):* Yeah, right. And your hips. But do you really like them?

MOTHER: *I* like them. But you don't seem to be sure. Do you feel good in them?

KATE: No, I'm going to wear my old black jeans. *(slams door; leaves happy)*

MOTHER *looks slightly dazed.*

Let's go to the videotape: It's not that Kate isn't asking about the jeans; she is. But she is really asking to be admired by her mother. Her mother tries to find something good to say. The trick is finding the thing you know and love about your daughter, something only a mother who's tuned in would say: her blue eyes, her freckles, how good she looks in a ponytail. A little positive attention will go a long way toward keeping the two of you connected. Just don't expect to sound smart, feel victorious, or have her thank you for your wisdom.

However you do it, keep the connection. Your daughter needs, although she doesn't know she needs, to have you around to help her work through the process of defining herself. Who better than you? After all, you are the one who knows her inside and out, who remembers who her true self is, and who can best remind her. You are her one true mirror of reality, support, and sanity. And if you can lend her your pink cashmere sweater, so much the better.

Intellectually, keep in mind that your daughter is in the process of separating, taking responsibility for her own body and becoming her own person. In that process, she feels herself to be entirely grown-up, not needing you at all. (Well, except for the sweater.) She's appalled that you consider her a child. She can see for herself just how much attention she's getting with her now highly visible feminine figure. She wants full control over her body and pushes you back because it's so threatening to have you think of her as a little girl. She's completely convinced that she understands exactly how the world works. She's ready to argue with your "distorted" worldview at the drop of a hat, beginning many of her conversations with "That may be how it was for you when you were my age, but it's not that way anymore." She often ends with "You just don't understand." Resist the temptation to laugh or be disdainful of her logic. Instead, appreciate and hold on to the idea that she is, in her own totally maddening way, trying to figure out how the world works and how she fits into it.

Most of all, do not give up. Frankly, many mothers do give up right around now. They feel as though they talk and their daughters don't listen, that they care and their daughters don't, that there is no relationship left. It isn't true. Look for vital life signs. If your daughter is still breathing, if she occasionally shows up at the dinner table, if she remembers your name, you still have a relationship.

It's easier to hold on and respond sensibly if you can understand why your daughter is acting particularly inscrutable or impossible. There's a reason for even the most unreasonable behavior:

- If your daughter is acting sullen or depressed, make sure that you don't get pulled into a depression with her. At the same time, don't make things worse by cutting yourself off from her.
- If your daughter won't talk to you or you get the silent treatment, it means she's angry and wants to make you feel bad; it's meant to bother you. Don't play the game. If you run after your daughter and try to get her to talk, she's succeeding in making you feel like you did something wrong. Instead, just figure out what you need to say to her, say it, and move on.
- If she acts hostile and bitchy, don't let yourself respond in kind. Call her on her behavior. Let her know how disrespectful it is, then tell her the kind of behavior you expect. Be specific about what you consider appropriate.
- If your daughter is oppositional and defiant, know that this kind of behavior is usually a cover for anger or fear that she isn't expressing verbally. Ask her what she's covering up with her attitude. If she won't volunteer what's really bothering her, venture what *you* think it is. Then she can correct you if she thinks you're wrong and maybe tell you what's up.
- If she's uncommunicative, closed off, or uncharacteristically shy, let her be. Just be observant and there for her, without intruding or prying. Don't ask her a million ques-

tions. Don't try to snap her out of it by offering unwanted help or suggestions.

- If she's secretive, respect her privacy. Be patient. She will eventually share more. And remember that the more you intrude, the less likely she is to open up. Also examine your own behavior. How open are you with your daughter? How much do you share with her?

- If she's never home, the bedroom door is always closed, or she's always on the phone or online, don't necessarily mistake her chronic absence for popularity. Your daughter is sending you a message and you have to figure out what it is. Her never being around may signal that she feels detached. It's important that you make it clear to her that she is an integral part of the family. And then you might need to set some rules for her—like Sunday dinner at home. If you don't question her about her absence, she might conclude you don't care or don't want her around.

- If she's alienated, if she makes it clear you don't understand her or much of anything, don't take it personally. You need to accept the fact that right now your daughter is resistant to your ideas and your worldview. She's also probably resistant to your cooking, your walk, your lipstick color. Don't argue with her about any of this. The best you can do is listen to what she has to say. Try to start conversations with her that are involving and animated, that let you both express ideas and opinions. Don't get so hurt by her resistance that you can't talk to her or that you feel like you don't want to deal with it.

- If she only comes to you for money and rides, let her know that a relationship is a two-way street. You can tell her point-blank, "You come to me only when you want money or need a ride. If you want me to do something for you, this is what I need *you* to do. This is what I expect . . ." And tell her specifically what that is.

- If anything you ask of her is a huge burden and you get lots of disdainful looks and rolling of her eyes, relax. This is normal resistance; feeling put upon by you sometimes makes your daughter feel above it all and separate. Don't argue, but do hold your ground. Be firm and clear about what your needs are and the needs of the family. Tell your daughter what you expect from her. Set limits and let her know that she has responsibilities.

TO BE REALISTIC, you should not aim too high or hope to change anything overnight. Small victories count. Don't bank on your daughter's being your witty dinner partner; your warm, empathetic friend; and your fun shopping pal. Don't expect it and don't even hope for it; it wouldn't be good for her or for you. The ultimate mother-daughter relationship is *not* the one where you say proudly, "My daughter is my best friend." We can trace the root of many body image issues to the confusion of who you are to your daughter and who she is to you.

When you're attached at the hip, it becomes difficult for your daughter to separate from you without feeling sometimes angry and often guilty. Because she truly loves you, feelings of guilt become intolerable to her. She feels like she can't express them, so she keeps them inside and winds up turning them against herself; and she expresses these powerful negative emotions through her body. This reaction opens the door for a whole range of body image problems that involve distortions of identity, sexuality, and self-esteem. Hello, depression. Hello, eating disorders. Helping your daughter separate from you to live her own life is the best gift you can give her.

As you initiate this eminently worthwhile process, remember that separation doesn't mean severing. You need to stay connected. And know that just about any connection is a good connection. For example, if your daughter wanders into the kitchen and mentions that the vegetables you cook are always mushy, and by the way, the jeans and T-shirts you wear are always frumpy, that's okay. Any connection can lead to a dialogue, and any dialogue can lead to a valuable listening and learning experience. She thinks the vegetables are mushy? Cook them al dente next time. She hates your clothes? Ask her to come with you to help you get a new outfit. Let your daughter feel that she matters, that you listen to her and value what she has to say. And guess what? She might do you the honor of keeping you on her radar screen, because the best way to be sure that she will listen to *you* and learn from *you* is to make sure that you listen to *her* and learn from *her*.

Part of the listening and learning process is being sensitive to her issues and her feelings. It's not easy to make things better, but you can start by not making them worse. Here are some things *not* to do if you want to keep the process going with your daughter:

- Don't start a conversation with "Why are you doing this to me?" or "How could you do this to me?" It's not about your suffering or her guilt. It's about talking so she'll listen. Start instead with something like "I don't understand what's going on."

- Don't say, "I don't understand what's the matter with you. I've asked you fifty times to hang up all those clothes on your bed." This will only distance her further. As neutrally as you can, state the problem and the consequences: "Your laundry has been on your bed for three days. If it's not put away by . . . , you won't be going to . . ."

- Don't announce, "I have much more experience than you do; I know what's best." Your daughter's not going to learn to think for herself if you run over her like a steamroller. Try something like "Tell me what you think. I'll tell you what I think. We'll figure out what's best for you and for everyone involved."

- Don't go on the defensive. If your daughter criticizes your diet advice, don't come back with "How dare you tell me that I don't know what I'm talking about? I've been on a hundred more diets than you have."

- Don't put on a front. Be yourself. If you feel angry, express your anger.

- Don't pretend to be perfect and suggest that you never

make mistakes. That only makes your daughter feel that if she is anything less than perfect, she's a failure.

- Don't manipulate. Don't try to get control by losing your self-control. When you cry or act like a drama queen about something, you just scare her. You might win this time, but you've lost all credibility with your performance.

- Don't call in the big guns. Just because you're struggling with something, don't threaten that you'll get her father or her school principal to deal with it.

- Don't compare her to her siblings or friends, and don't compare your relationship with her to some other, better mother-daughter relationship where the daughter is actually nice to her mother.

- Don't go silent. Don't leave her emotionally when you get angry with her. Not talking to her in order to show her just how angry you are or to make her feel guilty doesn't ever work.

- Don't blame her. Don't shame her. Saying something like "You complain all the time that you're too fat, but here you are snacking on chocolate fudge brownie ice cream" is not exactly a motivational strategy or a boost to her self-esteem.

- Don't even think of trying for a good comeback when she says, "Well, I didn't ask to be born." There isn't one.

- Don't ever bargain with your daughter, especially about body image issues. Don't say, "I'll make a deal with you. If you lose the ten pounds you need to, then I'll give you a hundred dollars." The effect of this kind of bargaining is extremely powerful. It makes your daughter feel betrayed by you. She thinks (correctly) that you're doing this for yourself, not for her. And she feels (also correctly) that you don't have respect for what she thinks about her weight issues.

Nurturing conversations and heart-to-heart talks aren't possible when your daughter feels you're clueless about who she is, when you're insensitive to her feelings, or when she's angry with you. They can be hard for you, too, especially when she says things that sound absurd or untrue or when she gives you an opinion from the person she considers a real expert, who turns out to be her friend Heather, age fifteen. How are you supposed to listen with a straight face? An example: "Mom, there's no danger at all in getting a tattoo. The guy wears rubber gloves and besides he went to tattoo school—*graduate* tattoo school—for years." Or she tells you that there's no way she could get hepatitis from the needle, because navy blue ink is the safest and that's what she'll use. Heather told her.

Your first instinct is to set her straight. Save your breath. What you need to do is identify the real issue and let her know you're taking it seriously. You've told her no tattoos, but she's faced with the fact that everyone around her is running off to get one and she's not sure where she stands and she's trying to figure out where *you* stand. Do you *really* mean no? Are you just saying there's a health risk? Is it that you don't want her to look grown-up? Feel sexy? Have a boyfriend? Most kids are trying to find out if you mean what you say.

They're testing. On a small note of reassurance: if your daughter were really convinced it was so safe and cool and right, she would just go off and do it. (More on how to handle that later.)

Read between the lines and realize that despite her arguing, she doesn't need to get her way. What she needs is to figure out what makes sense, and your job is to help her figure that out. At the same time that she's telling you how she feels, she's asking herself lots of questions: "Who am I?" "Is this me?" "What's best for me?" And always, "Is what I'm thinking of doing going to make me popular or get me a cute boyfriend?" She gets lost trying to figure out the answers. She blows things out of proportion; she experiences everything with equal intensity; she can't always see the forest for the trees.

So in the land of confused communication, you're convinced she's not listening to a word you're saying, but what you need to see is that she's overwhelmed. She's wrestling with this decision while being influenced by her friends' point of view, by magazines, by movies, by MTV. If you take the bait and try to win, you will be drawn into a competition as to who's right, who's wrong, who's smart, who's stupid. The unfortunate result is a power struggle. You feel misunderstood and miserable and miles apart; so does she.

So how do you handle a potentially explosive issue? Here are three examples of how to discuss with your daughter her desire for a tongue stud:

A month or two before her sixteenth birthday:

LINDSAY: I'm going to get a tongue stud when I'm sixteen, no matter what you say. I've wanted one since I was thirteen and you know it.

MOTHER AND FATHER *(anxious and unsure; trying to buy time and find a good argument):* You do? We know you talked about it, but we didn't know you were so serious. Frankly, we don't think it's a good idea.

LINDSAY: Well, it's not about you. You don't understand, anyway.

MOTHER AND FATHER: It's true. We don't understand. But we can see how important this is to you. So we'll check it out; we'll talk to the doctor and the piercing place to make sure it's safe. What if your tongue gets infected?

LINDSAY: Whatever. That's stupid. Everyone's got one.

On her sixteenth birthday:

MOTHER AND FATHER: We've thought a lot about piercing and we talked to Dr. Sherman. We think it's probably safe if you do it the right way. We don't know why, as an athlete, as someone who respects her body, you would want a stud in your tongue. But we realize that at the end of the day, it's your body and it's your choice. You're the one who has to live with it. But honestly, we'd prefer that you don't do it.

LINDSAY: Well, I'm getting it anyway. Next week, when I have a day off from school.

Two weeks later:

LINDSAY: If I didn't have all those tests to study for and that track meet, I would get my stud today!
MOTHER AND FATHER *(resisting temptation to rise to bait):* Uh-huh.

Two weeks later:

MOTHER: How are you feeling about it now?
LINDSAY *(distressed):* I'm wondering if it hurts.
MOTHER: I can't imagine it doesn't. But you know us. We're so uncool. We can't imagine why someone would put a hole in their tongue in the first place.
LINDSAY *(laughing):* You are *seriously* uncool.

A month later: No tongue stud . . . yet. Lindsay's parents have their fingers crossed. They try to avoid using words like pierce *or* tongue *in conversations with Lindsay.*

Lindsay's parents did a lot of things right. They widened their network and took some of the pressure off themselves by talking to other people, people with knowledge and authority. Lindsay never talked to the doctor herself, but she did ask her parents what the doctor said and took it into consideration. Because her parents didn't go crazy, because they took Lindsay seriously, because they didn't feel the need to get the last word, because they managed to comment without controlling, Lindsay didn't feel she had to race out and get pierced. Most important, they let her know that what she does to her body is her own responsibility.

But what if you say all the right things and your daughter still goes off and does it? When her message is a clear "So there"? What could Lindsay's parents have said then?

LINDSAY: So I decided to get pierced after all.

MOTHER AND FATHER: Well, we're not happy with it, but at the end of the day, it's your body.

If you find yourself in this situation, don't continue the war. It's done. Recriminations are not healthy for her or for you. Just give her a straight message about how you feel and move on.

In this next case, Gina's parents try to take control and lose, while sending all the wrong messages to their daughter about the boundaries of her body:

GINA *(insistent): Everyone* has a tongue stud.

MOTHER *(in a fake pleasant voice; actually a little scared of her daughter's anger and scared of piercing):* Oh, honey, not *everyone.* Debbie doesn't have a tongue stud.

GINA: Debbie is a total loser. It's legal in the city, so I'm going to get one this weekend, whether you like it or not.

MOTHER *(pleasantness dissolves; more frantic):* It doesn't matter if it's legal in the city, it's not legal in this house. I forbid you. And wait till I tell Daddy. *(She calls him in as the heavy.)*

FATHER: What are you, crazy?! No way! How could you even think of such a sick thing? *(voice rising)* You are never getting something that mutilates your body.

GINA *(getting hysterical):* Yes, I am! And it's not mutilation, it's body art.

MOTHER *(starting to cry):* You were such a beautiful baby.

GINA *(ignoring her):* You can't stop me. You don't care if I ever have a boyfriend.

FATHER *(enraged and determined to win at any cost):* This isn't about boyfriends. No daughter of mine is going to have a hole in her tongue. That's it! You're grounded if you do this. No allowance, no car.

MOTHER *(still crying; reverts to sweetness):* Honey, we just want to do what's best for you.

GINA *(screaming):* I hate you! And I don't care what you say! You don't love me. You're not parents, you're jailers! *(She runs out of room; locks herself in her bedroom. She calls all of her friends and starts plotting. She's more fiercely intent on getting her tongue pierced than ever.)*

In this case the parents' efforts to stop Gina from making a bad decision get derailed quickly when it becomes clear that Gina is not going to reflect back the choice her parents think she should make. When she doesn't, they dive right into the highly volatile issues of "Whose decision is it?" and "Whose body is it?" Gina, whose ideas about her body are her way of trying to separate from her parents, feels completely crushed. Her parents feel angry and helpless. In this power struggle, nothing constructive is said and nothing positive is achieved.

Any parent is vulnerable to being drawn into a struggle for control. But what do you do if you feel that your daughter isn't ever listening to you, let alone learning from you? That everything you say is falling on deaf ears? It's important for you to know that it isn't. The smart, sensible, supportive things you're saying to your bright and beautiful daughter will at some point click in. Not all of a sudden. Not in some dramatic way, as in a soap opera where the amnesia victim wakes up and suddenly everything is wonderfully clear. Your point of view will click with your daughter because you have stayed with this often painful long-term step-by-step process. Gradually she will internalize all the things that you've been saying to her and present them in her own voice. For the first time, your relationship will become a two-way street. She will really hear you, trust you, and talk to you. And she will see for herself that a positive connection with you actually leads to positive results for her.

So keep feeling that she's worthy. Keep having in-jokes between you; laugh at those punch lines that only the two of you find funny. Share yourself with her. Place importance on everything that matters to her. Think the best of her. Know that how you are together is as important as how you are apart. You will both be rewarded by a relationship that will keep you connected when you most need to be. Just don't expect to get your pink cashmere sweater back any time soon.

HOW TO KEEP THE PROCESS GOING

Pay attention to your daughter. Tune into the nuances of what she's saying. Not only will that help her know how much you care about her, it will help you understand things without having to ask her a million intrusive questions.

Talking isn't the only way to communicate; sometimes it isn't even the best way. Leave your daughter a voice mail, an e-mail, a Post-it Note, a note on her pillow. Saying less can be more effective than going on and on, and saying it in a note lets your daughter have a chance to think before answering you.

Don't worry so much. Constantly expressing your anxieties to your daughter makes her feel that everything is dangerous, while in reality taking risks and experiencing the world is one way for her to find herself. By restricting her too much, you're not just saying, "Don't explore, don't try new things." In effect you're saying, "Stay with me."

Accept responsibility for your mistakes. Let your daughter know that you're human, too.

You can roll with the punches without being a punching bag. Your daughter doesn't have to like what you say, but she has to respect it.

Don't be devastated unless something is really devastating. Keep things in proportion.

Talk about any conflict that's going on between the two of you. Don't bury it, but don't harp on it either.

Stay out of competition with your daughter, especially about who's fatter, who's thinner, who's lost more weight, whose jeans are looser.

Let your daughter express her feelings without expressing a judgment.

Work at staying involved with her. Talk about the things you're interested in; talk about her interests; develop things you can share.

If at first you don't succeed, try a different approach. Instead of saying, "Eat something healthy for a change," say, "I got your favorite yogurt. It's in the refrigerator."

Be smart. When your daughter asks questions like "Do I have to . . . ?" or "I don't understand why . . . ," tell her *exactly* what you need her to do. Come right to the point; don't get drawn into an endless and maddening "discussion."

Benign stupidity helps. You don't have to have an answer for every question. Let your daughter figure things out or look them up herself. She'll feel better about herself, and you won't feel like a human encyclopedia.

Chapter 4

TAKE A GOOD LOOK
AT YOURSELF

AS THE MOTHER of an adolescent girl, you need to ask yourself some important questions: How do you feel when *you* look in the mirror? How do you feel about your breasts, your weight, the lines around your eyes, your age? Listen to the voice in your head. Is it self-critical? Denigrating? Disparaging? Are you angry at yourself for going off your diet? Or are you so frustrated by endless dieting and calorie counting that you've just given up? Do you spend a lot of time thinking about what kind of plastic surgery you want to get? Are you obsessed with some aspect of your appearance? Do you feel that—no matter how mature you are about most things—these issues have been with you forever and will never leave?

These questions matter because *all* the body messages that you send your daughter, both spoken and unspoken, from the time she is a baby have a profound effect on how she feels about her body and herself. You are the person she most identifies with as a female. You are her primary role model. Even if she has a different body type from yours, if she is built like her father, if she's adopted, or if her father and you are of different races, *you* will still be the biggest influence on whether she develops a positive, healthy connection to her body.

Ultimately, how your daughter feels about her body depends on how you feel about your own. Strong intergenerational influences come into play here. As if in some sort of sorority you didn't know you had joined, certain beliefs, values, and perceptions are passed down in your family from one generation of women to the next. By conveying even the simplest messages to your daughter about attractiveness, thinness, beauty, popularity, and the right depilatory, you are passing down body image beliefs that have been woven into your consciousness. After a couple of generations, the things your mother said to you and that you say to your daughter, from "No one likes a fat girl" to "A woman never admits her age," become part of her female DNA. You present these statements and beliefs as facts to your daughter, and your daughter accepts them that way and gradually internalizes them as a part of her thinking.

Some of the most powerful intergenerational messages that you pass on are *un*spoken, not because they are secrets, but because they are unconscious. They are transmitted more as a subtext expressed in your behavior, your attitude, and your emotions. These messages are the anxieties, fears, and concerns so deeply rooted in your psyche that you don't even realize that they are there, let alone know that you are communicating them. They are, for example, the fears of the pregnant woman who doesn't feel beautiful, she only feels fat. The anxiety of a mother convinced that her chubby-cheeked two-year-old is overweight. The relief of a very fair mother who looks at her beautiful, healthy newborn daughter and skips right over the beautiful, healthy part to focus instead on her daughter's dark brows and lashes. "Oh, good," this mother thinks, "she won't need to worry about putting on mascara every day." At heart these fears and anxieties are all really one fear: that your daughter won't be pretty enough, thin enough, pleasing enough, to succeed in the world. The fear that no one will love her.

These unspoken messages are why we all tend to believe that fat is ugly and thin is beautiful. They aren't meant as criticisms or value judgments; they're well-intentioned beliefs, almost mythic in their stature, that come from an earlier time when women were powerless without beauty. What makes these beliefs so difficult to change is that they *remain* unspoken, are actively denied, never examined, and never put in their true perspective. The result is that, without even being aware of it, we're in danger of perpetuating the mantra of "pretty, thin, and pleasing" into yet another generation.

The inevitable consequence is a female peer pressure that quickly becomes part of every woman's body consciousness. This peer pressure isn't something you need Freud to explain. It's as simple as the fear of being different, of standing out, or of being gossiped about. It's the everyday kind of social pressure that makes women feel they need to listen closely to what people are saying. Think about it: You see a friend and in a microsecond you get or give a quick body check. *"She's gained so much weight, I hardly recognize her." "Look at her, she looks beautiful; did she have her eyes done or has she been working out?" "Can you believe how fat she looks in that spandex?"* What you're really hearing is that if you're not careful, your husband will find someone more attractive and desirable, your women friends will be gossiping about you at the gym, you might lose your job to someone younger and prettier. When women hear this constant commentary in their heads, it undermines whatever self-confidence they may have about themselves and their bodies. And these fears, taken to the extreme, make them feel that they simply don't have what it takes.

By the time you're grown up, you can't look in a mirror without knowing how profoundly all these influences have affected what you see and shaped who you are. From the day your daughter is born, you'll be bringing all of this to your relationship with her. You are the source from which she develops a sense of herself and her body. Your daughter takes you in in every way: visually, physically, emotionally. Initially she is attached to the pleasure of your body through your feeding and caring for her. And like all the other messages you give her, this immediate, intimate, and loving physical attachment gradually becomes internalized. In time your daughter learns how to comfort herself and take care of herself. This healthy balance of your care for her and her ability to care for herself forms the basis of a close, loving relationship between the two of you.

It's through your emotional and physical relationship with

your daughter that she first learns about body pleasure. Remember when she discovered her toes and managed to stick them in her mouth? When she learned to reach up to you from her crib to get picked up and held? When she discovered that she could open her mouth and make wonderful sounds? The joy you find in your infant daughter and the delight you take in *her* pleasure is the essence of her future self-esteem. It's how she gains a sense of her intrinsic value as a person.

So these early positive messages that you send her—that you find pleasure in her, that *she is a source of pleasure to you*— help her value her body and herself. Your daughter will take and transform your attention and care (mother love) into positive feelings about herself (self-love). Her body love develops from your nurturing and your soothing, from your hugs and kisses, from the physical comfort you give her.

When she was a baby, there was very little sleep but lots of kissing and cooing. As your daughter grew up, your early unconditional love for her turned into a love that is more conditional. Instead of seeing her as a sweet chubby baby, you see her asserting her own unique personality as she begins to become an individual. You stop responding to her adorable baby-ness and start responding to the reality of who she is and how she behaves. From early childhood on, you pick up clues from her about who she is and how she's feeling about herself. And your responses are so meaningful to her that she incorporates them into how she thinks about herself. She's a tomboy. She's a girlie girl who only wears dresses. Purple is the only color she'll wear. She's got to be the first in line for everything. She's a perfectionist and determined to be a star. She's your resident Cookie Monster. She couldn't care less about the applesauce stains from lunch on her T-shirt. In addition to guiding her, teaching her, and educating her, you now find yourself reacting to her and, in some subtle ways, trying to remake her by reinforcing only those qualities that you find desirable.

As a well-meaning mother who loves her daughter and wants only what's best for her, you no doubt tell yourself you're not *remaking* her, you're only *guiding* her. (As a rule of thumb, the minute you tell yourself that you "want only what's best for her," trouble looms.) You think that if you can mold her behavior and shape her values, you can protect her from acquiring bad habits and help prevent problems that could hurt her later. There is a danger zone here with flashing lights. The minute you overreach and transgress your daughter's boundaries, you stop guiding her and start controlling her. Instead of learning to please herself, she is given the clear message that she should be pleasing you. And that's not all. She sees your need to correct her behavior and micromanage her life as a vote of no confidence in her.

Your daughter needs the opportunity to learn from her choices and from her mistakes. She needs to figure out whether party dresses in the playground make sense. She has to decide for herself if the applesauce on her T-shirt is the end of the world or whether the color pink might not be just as pretty as purple. Understanding the difference between guiding and controlling is valuable when she is very young and once again when she's a teenager. Of course, now it's piercing and guys in rock bands instead of party dresses and purple. But it's still your job as a mother to balance her right to make her decisions and learn from her experiences with her safety and well-being. Even when she's legally an adult, your daughter needs you to set appropriate limits, be her mentor, and give her the right guidance.

Some mothers want to remake their daughters as a way of being close. They enjoy a sense of satisfying we-ness, a kind of "mommy and me" togetherness. You know who this mother is when you hear her say something like "It's so wonderful, my daughter and I have the exact same taste." Or, "Believe it or not, I can wear my daughter's clothes." Or, "I love to go to the gym with my daughter. We can take the same yoga class." The expression *too close for comfort* comes to mind.

So through all of her early years, in many different ways, you're letting your daughter know what you think and suggesting to her what she should think. And just when you think you know who she is and how to coexist with her, there she is teetering on the threshold of adolescence, where things change radically. She looks different, she acts differently, she starts to treat you differently. (When your daughter starts calling you by your name, not "Mommy," you know you're there.) Don't worry. All of who she is—her personality, her character, her likes and dislikes, her early experiences, good and bad—is still there. What is genuinely different now is how you have to respond to her. You need to mother and model and guide in a new and more intense way, and in some new areas: her sexuality, her changing body, her relationships with boys, her friendships.

Paradoxically, just at the moment when you can help your daughter most by being more involved, she is pushing you away. Remember that you're involved in a process. Remind yourself that although her pushing may be annoying and hurtful, you need to stay connected. It's this vital connection that allows you to send her the consistent, positive messages she needs to build a strong foundation for her health and well-being. When the ground under her feet feels a little shaky, that foundation becomes the one thing she can rely on.

While it is difficult to predict how your daughter will deal with her teen years, the type of relationship you have with her is an important determinant of how successfully she will deal with the tasks of adolescence. The better the emotional relationship and the stronger the foundation, the more likely it is that her adjustment will be a good one. Here are some questions that can help you see how your relationship with her may go, whether it will be easy or hard, whether it'll come naturally or you'll really have to work at it. (The questions are actually a lot like those "Is He Right for Me?" compatibility tests you used to take in women's magazines.)

Are the two of you a good fit? Is your daughter's personality and temperament something you understand? Or are you very different? Do you have a daughter who thinks she was born into the wrong family? Do you sometimes feel that you took the wrong baby home from the hospital?

❧

Were you able to connect with *your* mother when you were a teenager? Did you find that there was a generation gap between you? Did you feel so distant from her that you never wanted to tell her what was going on in your life? Do you just automatically assume that the same thing will happen with your daughter?

Aside from compatibility and intergenerational questions, there are questions about boundaries that can often predict whether your relationship will help your daughter separate from you and feel like her own person.

Do you overidentify with your daughter? Do you feel that what's happening to her is happening to you? Do you have unresolved body issues of your own? Do your concerns get enmeshed with your daughter's? Can you see which issues are yours and which are hers? Are you overly involved with her—to the point where you have a hard time pulling back from a conflict or find that you can't stop yourself from reading her diary or Internet journal? Do you feel that her behavior reflects on you to such an extent that you easily become humiliated by her or feel like rejecting her?

❧

Are you satisfied with your own life? Do you envy your daughter? Do you feel competitive with her?

In the best of all possible worlds, mothers would feel so good about themselves and their bodies—find such pleasure in them, experience them as so valuable and whole and strong, appreciate all their bodies do for them—that all their messages would be positive. In even an okay world, women would be able to keep a perspective on what really matters and what's really valuable. Well, welcome to a world where the media barrage women with the message that there is one stereotypical standard of ideal beauty (tall, thin, young, blond, busty) and that they don't come close to meeting that standard. Very few grown women are sixteen years old, six feet tall, with platinum blond hair and the body of a Victoria's Secret model. But that's only half the message. The other part promises women that if they just *cared* enough, *spent* enough, *tried* enough, there might be some hope after all. "Thin Thighs in 30 Days!" "Coming Up: Hollywood Plastic Surgeons Tell All!" "The First Crème That Visibly Reduces the Signs of Aging!" "The Anti-Cellulite Diet!" "Spring Makeovers—A New Body! A New Face! A New You!" "What's Keeping You from Being a Beauty?"

You can't change the entire culture, and you can't change who you are. You can't change what the media are saying, but you *can* change your own message. The message you need to give your adolescent daughter ought to be some variation on this: "Before you perfect the art of applying liquid eyeliner or lash-lengthening mascara, do what you need to feel good about yourself on the *inside*. Perfect your self-esteem and sense of who you are."

You can also help your daughter by filtering the media's

beauty myths. Don't believe that these messages are so powerful that you have no influence. Mothers who feel that they can't compete with these messages and who are too intimidated to say anything are selling themselves short. Talk about the myths. Get them out in the open. Admit how seductive these messages are to *all* women. Suggest your daughter read Naomi Wolf's book *The Beauty Myth*. In any way that works for you, tell her that she is not the sum of her body parts. Let her know that there's a difference between being enslaved to these ideas and having a sense of what is best for her.

Remember how crucial you are as a role model to her, and be vigilant about what messages *you're* buying into. Don't oversimplify things or assume a position of smug superiority. There's a difference between saying, "Oh, it's a commercial hoax. We shouldn't pay attention; we're above all that," and helping your daughter understand the relative value of pale pink lip gloss versus *her* value as a whole, thoughtful person. She needs to know that she has a choice; if she likes what she sees in *Vogue* or *In Style* and it makes her happy, then that might be what's best for her.

Explain to her that her expectations for something like a perfume or an acne cream need to be realistic. Tell her to go ahead and buy these products but keep in mind what they do and what they don't do. Perfume can make her smell wonderful and acne cream can clear up her skin (maybe). But they can't (even the expensive ones, even the giant-sized ones, even the ones a movie star endorses) make all her problems disappear. Take a note from the middle-aged mother who vividly remembers smoking her first cigarette at the age of fourteen and asking herself, "Hey, why isn't this cigarette making me sexy? Why is there no babbling brook like in the ad? Where are the handsome guys?" And of course the next question she had was not "What's wrong with the cigarette?" but "What's wrong with me?"

Keep mascara, Wonderbras, and no bras in perspective. It's not the end of the world if she wants to buy a Wonderbra or if she blows half of her allowance on face glitter or if she'd rather go to the mall than spend the day studying the causes of the French Revolution. She may spend two hours getting dressed and putting on makeup or change into twenty outfits to find the right one. Don't become so anxious about her that you police her. Use your judgment. You need to be able to say (and mean), "It's okay to take a break. It's okay to relax." Remember that spending three hours in front of the mirror contouring her lips will not keep your daughter from growing up to become a smart, caring, successful woman.

Sometimes the steps you need to take are very simple. In fact, there are only two things you need to do to start making any significant changes: become more insightful about yourself and listen carefully to your daughter. Knowledge is power. The more you understand yourself and the better you understand your daughter, the more effective you'll be in helping her. As you listen more carefully to her (and in chapter 5 we'll talk about *how* to listen), the discussions the two of you have will be more meaningful and the messages you both send and receive will be clearer. The result will be that she gets the quality of attention that all teenagers need from their parents. This attention is a delicate balance of caring, challenging, guiding, correcting, and disciplining which has as its aim something that every mother wants: the launching of her daughter into the world as a self-sufficient, self-contained, whole person who has respect for herself, for her body, and for others.

Help her understand that her comments and judgments about how she looks and what she's wearing and how much she weighs aren't just passing remarks. They become internalized to form her self-image, because adolescent girls, brilliant and complex though they may be, are still emotionally immature. This immaturity is what leads a girl to try out and act out all her feelings concretely. Instead of expressing them verbally, she expresses them through her body. She doesn't have to tell the world what and how she feels, she can *show* everyone instead. For her, this is a both necessary and satisfying solution. So you can actually read your daughter through her appearance and her actions. She's changing her clothes, her hairstyle, her hair color. She's going from blond to Goth, from gym socks to fishnet stockings—all to let you know that she's got a new depth and dimension, that she's more thoughtful and more emotional, and that she is suffering.

When your daughter has a problem, resist the temptation to place blame. This kind of thinking assumes that someone must have been "bad," otherwise the problem wouldn't have occurred. It doesn't help. You need to fix the problem, not blame. All the negative messages you send her—from how sloppily she dresses to how few friends she has, all the attention to how "bad" she is and the lack of praise for how "good" she is—are what sticks. If you make her feel really bad about her mistakes, she's likely to become defensive and turn you off. She will absorb what you've said (even if she won't let you know it at the time), but she won't be able to talk about it with you. And in silence your blame will turn into her shame.

Recognize your tendency to blame yourself. Not only is blaming yourself painful and nonproductive, not only does it keep you from moving forward, but also it has a far more insidious result. It's likely to make your daughter more angry with you than grateful. She'll think that you're so emotional and so needy that she has to be extraordinarily sensitive to your feelings. And when she's busy taking care of you, she's obviously not getting the help or guidance she really needs—from you.

If your usual message to your daughter is "I feel terrible. It's all my fault," or, "Oh, look, I've given you all these problems. How could I? Let me see what I can do," you're *not* helping. Worse, the longer your suffering continues, the more your daughter senses that somehow it's not even about her anymore: it's all about you. Now she's asking, "Can't this all be about *me*?" And here you thought you were helping her. Your daughter doesn't know what to do. She may vacillate between asking for your help and being angry. She may be enraged by your suggestions; the way she sees it, she hasn't even asked you for solutions. All she's asked for is attention, for you to listen to her.

The issues of blame and shame are expressed another way by the mother who channels her own blame into action. She feels compelled to either solve problems for her daughter or pressure her daughter to change her behavior. What lies beneath her overbearing "guidance" is a mother's anxiety and inability to separate. Offering your daughter support, not solutions, and letting her have problems and solve them on her own ultimately lets her feel good about her own abilities.

You matter most to your daughter because you are the one who, by your words and actions, can best help her become a woman who is capable of loving herself and loving others. By understanding who *you* are and taking the time to learn who *she* is, you will be able to read her correctly and react to her appropriately. By letting her in on the secret that all women wish they were perfect but know that they're not, by admitting to her that once in a while a good manicure is more spiritually uplifting than a Russian novel, by reminding her that you were the one (and the only one) who steadfastly supported her right to wear nothing but the color purple for months and months, you give your daughter the best possible shot at acquiring a healthy self-esteem and a positive identification with you as a woman.

"I HAVE MET THE ENEMY
AND SHE IS ME"

Wonder why your daughter can't find a positive thing to say about her body? Listen to how you talk about yourself, what you say to your friends, or the "humorous" asides you make. If you relate to your body as the enemy, so will your daughter.

❧

"How many calories do you think that muffin had? Don't tell me the truth or I'll kill myself with the butter knife."

"I'm never eating again."

"I can't believe you let me eat that."

"A cookie? What are you trying to do? Make me fat?"

"My weakness for cheesecake is a sin."

"I just look at the menu and I gain weight."

"I might as well apply this ice cream directly to my hips."

"No, really. I haven't had a cookie since 1972."

"I remember when I used to have a waist."

"I'm made up of mismatched parts. What God had left over, he gave me."

"The reason that I like to shop for shoes is that it's the only time I don't feel fat."

"I wish I had the money for liposuction."

WHAT HAPPENS WHEN YOU DON'T RESPECT YOUR DAUGHTER'S BOUNDARIES, OR "WHOSE PROM IS IT, ANYWAY?"

You felt fat and dowdy at your prom, so you're determined that your daughter will feel like a movie star at her prom.

Don't project your feelings onto her. It's her prom, not yours. Let her decide how she wants to feel.

~

You take her to five different stores and make her try on everything. If she's going to be a star, she's got to have the perfect dress.

Don't be so involved with her. Don't try to control her. Get a life.

~

Then she tells you she doesn't even want to go to the prom. You say, "What do you mean, you don't want to go to the prom? Proms are the most important part of high school and you'll regret not going for the rest of your life. By the way, I made you an appointment to get your hair done that morning."

Don't overreact. Don't grill her with a million intrusive questions. Don't sulk. Don't try to bribe her into going.

~

She goes to the prom. You stay up all night waiting for her to come home and tell you everything. She tells you nothing.

You're too enmeshed with your daughter. Go find a friend your own age. And if you really want to find out how it went, don't ask your daughter, ask one of her friends who likes to talk.

Chapter 5

"YOU HAVE TO SAY I'M PRETTY, YOU'RE MY MOTHER"

EXACTLY WHY IS IT so incredibly hard for mothers and adolescent daughters to talk to each other? Why do you feel like you always say the wrong thing? Why does she feel like you haven't heard a word she's said? What are the language barriers in this foreign land where exchanges that used to be so clear and logical are suddenly incomprehensible? Well, how much time do you have? Just kidding! But there are a lot of different reasons.

First of all, mothers and daughters are often at cross-purposes, and as a result, they really *are* speaking two different languages. There's a language problem and there's a hearing problem. However well you attempt to communicate with your daughter, she's likely to be so overwhelmed by the number of changes—both internal and external—she's experiencing that she can't even hear what you're saying, much less give you a reasonable response. And the brighter and more sensitive she is, the more thoughts she's trying to process. The good news is that later on, when she's slightly older, her complex thinking will serve her well, but for now she's filled with contradictions and conflicts. The end result is that she's so overwhelmed with ideas, so flooded with what she's feeling and experiencing, that she has no way of sorting things out and putting them in perspective, let alone articulating them.

Besides, she doesn't really *want* to. When they become adolescents, girls naturally want to keep their most private thoughts to themselves. You can be the world's most open and accepting mother, and your daughter will still not share her thoughts with you; her need for privacy is greater than her need to confide in you. This reserve is actually an important element of her healthy adolescent development. She needs to establish a boundary between you so that she can separate from you and begin to assert her independence. This is the time when her phone conversations are whispered, doors are shut, and she decides to write everything in her private journal.

Amazingly, you find that you're one of the few people she *won't* talk to. She'll talk to strangers, friends, teachers, counselors, grown-ups she's just met. If she used to talk to you, she's now pretty much stopped. If she never talked much, any conversation she engages in with you is likely to be strident and argumentative. And however certain you are that if she just gave you a chance, you would understand and accept her unconditionally, her need to separate is too intense for her to approach you.

She's stopped talking to you not because she doesn't love

you, but because she experiences you as someone very powerful. She must push you away very hard to feel that she is her
own person. Ironically, the closer and more important your
relationship has been, the harder she is likely to push and the
more vocal she is likely to be in her constant assertions that
you're powerless over her and can't tell her what to do.

So what happens when you want to talk and she doesn't?
It's not a pretty picture. Every conversation becomes a potential argument. Or you say something and your daughter says,
"Leave me alone." You could have what's called *cross-
communication*. (You know it's a real problem when shrinks
have given something its own name.) Cross-communication
happens when you say apples and she says oranges; you say,
"That skirt's too short," and she says, "I have nothing to
wear"; you say, "I don't like you to go out without telling me
where you're going," and as she opens the door to leave with
her friends, she says, "We're not going anywhere."

You might find yourself in a *negative feedback loop*, which is
really just a fancy name for those maddening conversations
where you both keep going round in circles getting nowhere.
This is the kind of frustrating interaction you have when your
daughter wants to distance herself, so she offers negative and
obscure information. You pursue her, trying to get clarifica-
tion, but she resists revealing more. Your daughter is happy
being unhappy and making you unhappy, too: these conversations justify her helplessness and adolescent sense of victimization. They're even more satisfying to her because they let
her feel that it's all your fault. Negative feedback loops are

most likely to occur when your daughter is enmeshed with you and doesn't feel whole without you.

DEBBIE: I feel fat.

MOTHER: You're not fat.

DEBBIE: You don't know what you're talking about.

MOTHER: Of course I do, and who knows better? I'm your mother.

DEBBIE: That's just it! You have to say I look good because you're my mother.

MOTHER: That's not true. You look so skinny in those jeans.

DEBBIE: These are my fat jeans. You don't know anything.

MOTHER: Thin jeans, fat jeans—you look fine.

DEBBIE: Fine? That's all I look? *Fine?*

MOTHER: *Fine* means good. *Very* good. Beautiful.

DEBBIE *(disgusted):* Look at my butt. Unless you're blind, my butt doesn't look "very good."

MOTHER: Why are you always putting yourself down?

DEBBIE: You just don't understand.

And on and on and on.

Besides all the varieties of negative communication, you can have *false* communication. This happens when your daughter tells you what she thinks you want to hear. No matter how hard you try, she won't let you in, so she just placates you. It's part of her being defensive and wanting to guard her privacy. She's scared that being open with you would put her at a strategic disadvantage and threaten her independence. Moreover, she can't imagine that you would listen to her sympathetically. Maybe the following conversation sounds familiar:

MOTHER: Are you okay? You look so sad.

JANET *(annoyed)*: I'm fine.

MOTHER: You look kind of down today.

JANET: No, I just have a lot of homework.

MOTHER: Well, the phone hasn't been ringing. Is something going on with your friends?

JANET: I see them at school. And everyone's got a lot to do.

You find yourself pursuing her and once again she responds by distancing herself from you. The result is that you find yourself talking to the back of her head as she walks out of the room.

It's not just your daughter's need to stop talking or your herculean efforts to keep talking that leads to problems. Adolescence is not the Age of Reason. It is, however, the Age of Whatever or Just Because. You say, "I don't understand why you always feel so bad about yourself," and she stops the conversation with "Just because." You say, "Don't you want to wear a sweater over that little tank?" and she says, "Whatever." You ask what happened on the date she previously couldn't stop talking about, and she announces, "I don't want to talk about it."

The things that really matter and make sense to your daughter at this age are quantifiable: her weight, her clothing size, the number of boyfriends she has had, how many zits she has on her face. Well-meaning doesn't cut it and a compliment can just as easily be taken as an insult.

MOTHER: You look beautiful in that outfit.
ZOE: No, I don't. I look stupid. And you're just saying that because you're the one who wanted me to buy it.

Feel like giving up? Don't. (This might be a good time to reflect that someday your daughter will probably have children of her own; maybe she'll have an adolescent daughter—one just like herself.) Since part of the process is keeping the lines of communication open, you need to learn a new way to communicate. If you want to have any conversation at all, you need to examine what language you're speaking and learn the one your daughter is speaking.

Giving her a compliment, for example, is still possible. If you understand the paradoxical nature of your daughter's thinking and some tricky teenage psychology, you'll understand why she reacts the way she does. Your daughter wants compliments, but she can't quite accept and trust them because accepting a flattering comment threatens her separation from you. She does, however, need to hear positive feedback. As Freud would say, Go know. Even though you'll want to pull your hair out, here are some ways to give your daughter positive feedback and live to tell about it:

• Disarm her by starting with a disclaimer: "I don't expect you to believe me," or, "I'm just your mother, what do I know?"

- Don't give her a million compliments all at once: "What a gorgeous dress; I love your hair; you're so pretty; what adorable earrings." Too many at once makes them meaningless.
- Tune in to her feelings so that you can pick something to compliment that you know your daughter is really proud of.
- Don't give her a bogus compliment. "You look just like the girl on the cover of *Allure*, only you're prettier." She knows when you're faking it.
- Compliment something that has nothing to do with her features. "You have the most graceful walk; you always have."

While you are improving your language skills and perfecting the art of the compliment, don't expect that your daughter is doing the same thing. Her language is likely to be mostly nonverbal, expressed through her body. What she's thinking and feeling goes straight into action. She experiences her emotions physically: she feels jittery or she has a stomachache or she feels weird, as when she tells you that all of the hair on her body is going the wrong way. She feels fat—*fat* being the all-encompassing buzzword for her negative emotions. And all this concern about fat tends to coalesce in some struggle with food. Girls can undereat or overeat. They become vegetarians. They're fat-o-phobic. They're always starving. They're never hungry. Once they have articulated their feelings in their body, the problem is solved for them. Pointing to something specific that they think is wrong is a way to gain control over whatever is bothering them.

Food equals fat. Fat equals loss of control. Loss of control equals still feeling like a little girl. Still being a little girl means still being dependent on your mother and not feeling strong enough to depend on yourself. This formula leads to self-loathing, self-deprecation, and, at its most extreme, the possibility of some form of self-destruction. You can help your daughter deal with her feelings. No matter how hard she is struggling, she will mature by learning to put them into words. When she is able to organize her thoughts, she no longer has to act things out; she can think about something, mull it over, integrate it, make sense of it, and talk about it.

Communicating with your daughter doesn't just mean understanding her. It means understanding yourself and understanding what you're expressing. Too often mothers think they are having the most meaningful and heartfelt dialogue when they aren't even remotely connecting.

For example, there's the mother who talks *at* her daughter, not to her. When her daughter brings up a problem—the daughter thinks, for example, that her stomach is too flabby—her mother, always on a diet herself, couldn't be more empathetic. "Let's sit down and really talk about it," says the mother, who then proceeds to do all the talking herself. Fifteen minutes later, after lots of motherly advice about exercise and toning, about protein diets versus carb diets, she says to her daughter, "Now, don't you feel better?" And the girl, who has hardly said a word, looks at her mother stunned.

Then there's the mother who is constantly correcting—who sees every conversation as an opportunity to teach and guide. She sees her daughter as her own personal work in progress:

MOTHER: So, did you return that call?

EMMA: No, I'll do it later.

MOTHER: Don't do it later; you have to do it immediately. If you don't, it's rude. What will people think of me, raising a daughter who doesn't return phone calls?

There's the mother who tunes out her daughter's choices. She's too threatened to really listen:

VICKY: I'm going out for a sleepover at George's.

MOTHER: Who's George?

VICKY: Just a guy I know who used to go to my school. Now he's got his own apartment.

MOTHER: Okay. Just be home early.

There's the mother whose style of communication is so different from her daughter's that she and her daughter keep missing each other's signals. This mother may read her daughter's exuberance and loud girl talk as unfeminine and unbecoming. She wonders why her daughter always seems to call attention to herself:

ELIZABETH *(giggling and excited):* Omigod, the cutest boy in my class just called for a ride to school! I am so excited I could just die!

MOTHER: No boy is going to like you if you're that loud.

It's amazing how quickly you can reach an impasse when you're desperate to get a conversation going but more eager to present your own agenda than to listen. Once you're really ready to listen, here are some basic ways to turn a lose-lose communication into something a lot closer to win-win:

Stick to the issue.

❦

Decide what you hope the outcome of your conversation will be. Be clear with your daughter about it. Don't be too ambitious.

❦

Quit while you're ahead. One of the biggest mistakes you can make is, once you have a captive audience who is actually listening, to pile it all on—too many topics, too many issues, too many opinions.

❦

Remember, every conversation you have is a negotiation.

❦

Be aware that all conversations have some aspect of give-and-take. If you know that it's all about negotiation, you won't get upset thinking that your daughter is trying to put something over on you.

❧

Don't overreact. When she's overreacting, do whatever you can to defuse the situation.

❧

Don't retaliate.

❧

Don't make power plays and threats.

❧

Give your daughter your full attention while she's talking.

❧

If you're both angry and upset, do not bring up every other issue you can think of. Don't turn "Clean up your room" into a harangue about sex, boys, driving, and grades.

❧

Don't ask loaded questions. Tell your daughter what you need to know in order to help her or in order to have a conversation that won't leave you feeling like you need a stiff drink. Be simple and direct: "How can I help you?" or, "Can you tell me?" or, "I can't help you unless you tell me what's going on."

Lists are easy. Real life is harder. Applying any advice to a real daughter in a real situation takes a little more understanding and insight. Here are some communication principles that might help when you feel that the two of you are in a rut or on different planets.

YOU'RE ALWAYS TALKING AT CROSS-PURPOSES.

You're each so busy trying to make your point that you're not hearing each other. Stop talking. Stop trying to make your point. Ask your daughter to stop talking, too. Say something like "We're getting nowhere. Let's stop." Suggest, "Tell me what you think I'm saying, and I'll tell you what I think you're saying. And then tell me if I've got it right." Essentially, rewind the tape, replay it, and correct it. Give your daughter a chance to correct it, too.

WHAT IS SHE SAYING? ARE YOU SPEAKING THE SAME LANGUAGE?

When there seems to be a real language barrier, you can deconstruct and decode if you provide a reality check. Confront your daughter (nonaggressively) as if you were holding up a mirror to reflect what she's saying. Say to her, "This is what I think I hear you saying." If she agrees, take the next step. Then clarify the meaning of what she is saying by putting it in context. Say, "When you say this, it relates to all these issues, and so this is what it all means to me." If she's still nodding, go on to interpret the issue and its meaning. If she sees it the same way, then you can have a real discussion and understanding.

SHE WON'T TALK TO YOU ABOUT IMPORTANT ISSUES; EVERYTHING FROM SCHOOL TO SEX TO HER SOCIAL LIFE IS OFF-LIMITS.

Recognize that there are delicate and ever-changing conversational boundaries in adolescence; your daughter may tell you everything on Monday and then nothing on Tuesday. Be prepared for ups and downs, sharing and withholding. Be prepared to say, "It looks like you're not in the mood to talk. Tell me later if you want to." (Do not interrupt her ten minutes later, asking "So, ready to talk?") Know that most issues that are really important will come up again and again, so you always have another chance. Also, accept the fact that even the sincerest mother-daughter heart-to-heart talk won't always be enlightening or profound. Knowing this, you won't feel disappointed after a talk, and your daughter won't feel that she's disappointing you.

When she does talk, don't be judgmental about whatever she says. Hold off on your tendency to give a color commentary ("You did *what?* He said *what?*") on what she shares with you.

It's often useful to end a conversation, think about it, then later say, "I was really interested in what you had to say about . . ." Or find a book or movie that relates to what the two of you were talking about. This way, conversation stops being a command performance and starts to be something far more organic to your relationship.

If you can do all these wise, motherly things, you'll reduce the tension your daughter feels and you'll find that the two of you have more pleasurable conversations. The more conversations you have, the more these sensitive issues will just start coming up. So don't expect to sit down when *you* want to and have the Big Talk with your daughter. (In fact, try to avoid initiating Big Talks.) You'll find that big topics are all part of a long thread that continues through your daughter's adolescence. You don't need to accomplish everything all at one time.

You'll know you're succeeding when you have fewer conversations that begin with her saying, "Buy me . . . ," "Drive me . . . ," "Give me . . . ," "Get me . . ." Conversations will be more engaging and rewarding for both of you. You will start to be more mother as person and less mother as credit-card-service provider.

DON'T LOSE YOUR SENSE OF HUMOR.

The tension that pervades your relationship with your daughter can easily extinguish the natural humor, joking, and teasing that's such a necessary part of a family relationship. It's easy to forget how to laugh at yourself. And your daughter is so supersensitive that it's hard for her to laugh at herself. You both need to find ways to lighten up a little.

IS THIS A CONVERSATION OR AN AMBUSH?

She's got an agenda and she wants you to answer yes or no to something *instantly*, and you don't even know what she's asking you. A reminder: the adolescent clock is on Teen Time, which is to say, everything is *immediate* and *urgent* and *important* and in *italics*. To your daughter you are simply an obstacle that she has to get through. Your daughter: "Mom, when Calley comes over, can we both go to the mall and then exchange the dress you didn't like for the coat you said you wanted me to get and that other dress instead? I need to know *right now* because Calley's mother is waiting. Bye."

These conversations come at you out of the blue. They sound like your daughter is asking permission, but she isn't, really. They also sound like maybe she didn't actually start at the beginning of the sentence or else you missed some essential part of what she said.

If you feel blindsided, be clear about what you're feeling. Tell your daughter to slow down. Don't feel as if you have to produce the answer right away. Most teenage girls will respond with impatience, but you can say, "Look, I'm going to keep an open mind, but I can only give you an answer once I understand what you're talking about. You have to tell me more."

Your not having the instant answer to everything is good for both you and your daughter. Asking her for more and better information forces her to take more responsibility for her requests; she has to work harder to clarify her request, to articulate it, to persuade you to say yes to it. The more you understand what she's really asking, the less likely you are to feel ambushed.

Some issues are so difficult for both of you to talk about

that they go way beyond any helpful guidelines. They are so potentially volatile that we call them *Landmine Topics*. You can spend lots of time trying to think of the perfect answer; there isn't one. With these topics, it's going to be a difficult and uncomfortable discussion no matter what.

Here are some of the most common:

- Your daughter doesn't just *think* she's overweight, she really is.
- Your daughter is noticeably underweight and involved with some sort of extreme and unhealthy dieting.
- Your daughter is painfully shy; social situations are pure torture for her.
- Your daughter has a real problem with something that has to do with boys, dating, sex, or her sexual orientation.
- Your daughter is doing something that really alarms you, like body piercing and tattoos, and you're worried about infection and scars. Or she is engaging in drug or alcohol use and you have a family history of addiction.

If you are in one of these situations, first acknowledge that it exists. Do not be overwhelmed by fear, but also realize that it will not go away by itself. If you're comforting yourself by saying, "Oh, it's just a stage," you're not just being less than candid with yourself, you're letting your daughter down by not dealing with the issue.

The best way to deal with a Landmine Topic? If your daughter *could* talk about her problem, she *would*. But she can't. And she doesn't want to let you talk about it either.

As a mother, you feel pressure because you simply want to help her, and there is often pressure from other people in your family who see how your daughter is struggling and who expect *you* to solve the problem. But no matter how much your daughter may try to keep you in the dark about a serious issue, it will surface. While she may not bring it up, you'll see it in the way she's acting or you'll hear it in the feedback she's getting from her teachers, her guidance counselors, her friends, the mothers of her friends. Be alert to these signs and warnings. Once you're sure your daughter is aware of them, too, you can more easily bring up the problem and confront the situation in a clear, unemotional way.

Once the problem surfaces on its own, it's easier for your daughter to see you more as her ally than as her critic. While there is no one way to go about solving the problem, you can be helpful by not becoming so emotionally overwhelmed that you make both of you feel worse. Your goal is to be both empathetic and straightforward about what you see happening. You need to confront your daughter with the reality that (a) a real problem exists and (b) if she tries to run away from it, things will only get worse. Let her know that you're ready to help if she's ready to deal with it.

Start by listening to what your daughter says and by being sensitive to her needs and her fears. If she isn't ready to have a conversation about her problem and you force it, the conversation is going to go nowhere. Harping on the problem will just lead to fights or drive her away, and all your reassurances, suggestions, and solutions will fall on deaf ears. Often these problems have ratcheted up to Landmine status because your daughter's attempts to deal with them in the past have been unsuccessful.

Let her know that being alone with her problem may be one of the reasons she feels as bad as she does and that sharing it will make it easier. Suggest that if she's been sharing her distress with her close friends, they may have been helpful to her in some ways but not in all the ways she needs. Tell her you know that her first instinct is that you will be critical of her or disappointed in her once she does share her problem with you. Let her know that she's projecting *her* feelings onto *you;* what she thinks you'll feel is coming from her own self-critical feelings. Make it clear to her that while she may have given up or be living with a self-defeating solution (like starving herself or withdrawing socially), it's not a real solution and sooner or later she will be as hurt by the solution as she is by the problem itself.

Give your daughter other options. If she is too embarrassed or reticent to talk to you, let her know that's okay. Help her widen the net. Suggest other smart, sympathetic people she can talk to—relatives, friends, neighbors, special teachers, clergy, or other counselors. The bottom line is, the more she's talking, the more likely it is that she'll eventually talk to you.

No matter what happens—no matter how big or small a problem is, no matter how astute and brilliant your approach to it is, don't expect your daughter to follow the script:

PATTY: I'm so fat.

MOTHER: What's *really* bothering you, honey?

PATTY: Just because I know I'm fat doesn't mean something is bothering me. *(Door slams.)*

Or:

ILONA *(cheerful):* I'm not so worried about being fat.

MOTHER *(thrilled):* Wow, that's great!

ILONA: It just doesn't bother me so much anymore.

MOTHER *(more thrilled):* Really?

ILONA: Yup. Because I realized that I'm so ugly, it doesn't really matter whether I'm fat or not.

When words fail and rational conversation seems impossible, all you can really do is acknowledge your daughter's thoughts and feelings. By saying very little but continuing to be tuned in, by trying to figure out what's really bothering her and to decode what she's *really* saying, you'll at least maintain a connection. And it's always worth using your good instincts to hazard a guess about what's going on. Don't get thrown off if she rejects it. Your suggestion may help open up communication between you. And don't play Sherlock Holmes. If your daughter thinks you're trying to outsmart her with your detective work, she will understandably be resentful and more suspicious of you. You'll damage your relationship.

Communication skills, as difficult as they may be to achieve, are essential for your daughter to learn if she is to develop into a healthy, mature young woman, capable of functioning in the real world. Her ability to resolve conflicts and negotiate her needs originates in her relationship with you. And what your relationship with your daughter depends on, both now and in the future, is the ability to talk to each other. As she separates from you, her need for physical closeness, protection, and shelter will diminish. But what she *will* need more than ever is the ability to communicate. Maintain good communication, continue to develop trust, and a loving, caring relationship with your daughter will be your reward.

WHAT TO SAY TO HER IF YOU NEVER WANT HER TO TALK TO YOU AGAIN

"Wouldn't you be more comfortable if you got that in a larger size?"

"Well, if you didn't want to go off your diet, why did you order that pie à la mode at lunch?"

"Your friend Kathy is lucky. She's naturally skinny."

"Thank goodness you have a great personality."

"I didn't force you to eat that. You're gaining weight on your own."

"What shade would you say your hair is? I'd say mousy brown."

"If the saleswoman shows you something in spandex, just say no."

"I think you're ready for electrolysis. I wouldn't know, but it doesn't hurt a bit."

"You lose fifteen pounds and those hip huggers are yours."

"Size 2, size 12—it's just a number."

THIS CONVERSATION IS GOING NOWHERE, OR
HOW TO MEAN WELL AND MAKE IT WORSE

You try to comfort your daughter by pointing out what she can't change. "Oh, honey, don't fight it. Piano stool legs run in the family." "There's no two ways about it, you have the stubby O'Brian nose."

You present criticism as helpful advice: "Blue eye shadow isn't in." "You'd be so much prettier if your hair wasn't in your eyes."

You share offhand "observations" with her. "Look at that girl trying on that bikini. Disgusting! She's much too fat to wear something so revealing." Or, "We're definitely not buying those jeans. They make your butt look like a buffalo."

Your compliments are strictly backhanded: "You look good, but it wouldn't hurt you to lose a few pounds and get a decent haircut; you would feel *so* much better." Or, "That's such a pretty skirt. Well, it would be on a girl who wasn't quite so hippy." Or, "Now, that's an adorable sundress; it's a shame you can't wear that."

You sprinkle your conversation with magnanimous gestures: "You know, in just ten minutes my hairdresser could give you a couple of gold streaks to perk up the color—and it's my treat." "I just remembered that you can get a free makeup lesson at the department store this Saturday. It might be fun!"

You sneak the criticism in, in the kind of seemingly random double message only a mother could come up with: "It's the person you are inside. Eat a fruit." Or, "It's the content of your mind. Did you eat any junk food today?" Or, "It's most important to be kind. What's that on your face?"

You kill or maim with kindness. "Finally you have an outfit that looks good on you. Why don't you wear it tomorrow when there'll be more people over to see you?"

Chapter 6

WHAT KIND OF MOTHER ARE YOU?

THE BEST WAY to understand your daughter's behavior is to take a good look at your own. Read the slightly exaggerated, larger-than-life archetypes of mothers we've put together in this chapter and see if any part of them reflects your style. In each one, the mother is doing something that gets in the way of open, trusting communication with her daughter. These portraits are not very flattering, but be reassured: even the best mother has *some* element in common with one or more of these archetypes. (Only Joan Crawford has all of them.)

THE COMPETITIVE MOTHER

The competitive mother sees her daughter's adolescence as a threat. Her daughter's youth and vibrancy remind her that she's no longer young. Her daughter's budding sexuality makes it clear that pretty soon her daughter will be the one who is turning heads. It's this competition, sometimes overt, sometimes beneath the surface, that propels the competitive mother into a battle with her own body. Paradoxically, just at the time when she should be mature enough to feel comfortable with herself, she's on extreme diets, buying exercise machines, and flirting with her daughter's boyfriends. Living in a relentlessly youth-obsessed culture, she is faced with the fact that no matter how many hours she spends on the treadmill at the gym or how much money she spends on an anti-aging retinol cream, she's not going to turn back the clock. This is the kind of mother who says to her daughter, "When I was your age, I had so many boyfriends, I never sat home on Saturday night," or whose helpful advice runs along these lines: "If you would lose some weight, I bet a boy would call you, too." Or, "I bought these new jeans for you. I liked them so much I got a pair for me. Of course, I got a smaller size." Or, "You're awfully young to be getting cellulite."

THE MERGED MOTHER

This mother hasn't gotten over her own (usually unhappy) adolescence and sees herself in all of her daughter's experiences. If her daughter is the prom queen, this mother feels as if *she's* the prom queen. If her daughter fails a math test, *she's* failed a math test. And if her daughter is in some crisis, her mother feels like it's happening to her.

SARAH: Michelle was so mean to me today in school. She made fun of my new haircut in front of the whole class. I almost cried.

MOTHER: That is so awful. She is the most hateful girl. I
    never liked her. Just stay away from her.

SARAH: I actually did cry a little. I hate her.

MOTHER: I'm going to say something to her mother.

Next day:

SARAH: Oh, and Michelle invited me to sleep over at her
    house on Friday night after the football game.

MOTHER: Michelle? You like *Michelle?!*

A Merged Mother might encourage her daughter to try out
for the lead in the school musical. Then when her daughter
fails to get the part, she says (and really believes), "Well, no
wonder you didn't get the part. This school always picks the
same kids for productions." She only dimly gets it when her
husband points out that maybe the school picks the same kids
because they are the most talented.

This mother sees her daughter as an extension of herself.
Her mission is to save her daughter from the painful experiences *she* went through as a teenager. Suffering from her own
body image issues, this mother has developed a "body perfect" mentality, so she finds herself becoming anxious when
she sees her daughter gaining weight or getting zits. She'll say
things like "Do you think you really need that brownie?" or,
"I'm so full, aren't you?"

The Merged Mother so closely identifies with her daughter that she worries for *both* of them; she's unable to provide a
much needed reality check. Setting limits and knowing where
boundaries should be is hard for her. This is the mother who

would break her budget to buy her daughter something expensive because "everyone cool is wearing it." This is the mother who encourages her daughter to make friends with the in-crowd, the mother who would lie to her husband about where their daughter was going because she couldn't stand her missing a big rock concert or hot party. This mother can't tolerate the idea that her daughter would have anything other than a perfect life. Instead of *guiding* her daughter, she *colludes* with her.

THE ANXIOUS MOTHER

The turmoil of her daughter's adolescence has caused this mother to lose her bearings. She's on an emotional seesaw, constantly off balance. As much as she loves her daughter, her love is out of kilter; anxiety overwhelms her and her good instincts abandon her. She's so concerned about protecting her daughter that she worries too little or too much, often about the wrong thing. This is the mother who babies her daughter one day and on another day thinks she can be trusted to navigate the globe. She wants to help her daughter memorize her world history facts one day and the next day agrees to let her go with her older college friend, José, to visit his relatives in the Yucatán.

The Anxious Mother becomes extremely upset by her daughter's self-criticism. She's so anxious herself that she can't tolerate any of her daughter's negative feelings. Instead of listening, she is so determined to eliminate each and every one of her daughter's problems that she's unable to be empathetic. The most she can offer in the way of help is a kind of meaningless reassurance. Ironically, the end result is that her daughter feels her mother doesn't know who she is and that she doesn't care. And this mother, who cares very much, ends up alienating her daughter.

WENDY: I look terrible today.

MOTHER: Oh, no, you look just beautiful.

WENDY: Well, I don't feel beautiful.

MOTHER: Get your hair cut. I'll make an appointment. You can get your nails done, too.

WENDY: Forget it. Why would I want to go there? It's nothing but mirrors.

MOTHER: Have some ice cream. You'll feel better.

The Anxious Mother has three main subtypes:

The Counterphobic Mother: Counterphobic means responding to feelings of fear by doing the opposite. The child who is afraid of spiders grows up and gets a pet tarantula, for example. This mother is often unaware of her fears; she has a hard time knowing her own feelings and trusting her judgment, like the mother who earlier let her daughter zip off to the Yucatán without giving it a second thought. Without knowing it, this mother may so want to please her daughter and not upset her that she goes along with her in ways that fail to set appropriate limits.

The Hover/Smother Mother: True to her name, she is there

front and center. She is the lioness to her daughter's cub. There is no teacher this mother hasn't argued with, no squabble with her daughter's best friend that she hasn't intruded on, no fight with her husband in which she hasn't defended her innocent baby. This is the mother who's over-everything: overprotective, overinvolved, oversensitive.

She would be shocked to know that her fiercely loving stance is actually extremely controlling and undermines her daughter's growing sense of competence. This mother is afraid that as her daughter grows up, she herself will be out of a job, so she sets herself up as someone her daughter can't live without. This mother wants her daughter to stay a baby because babies love their mommies most. Her daughter inevitably concludes that she is helpless and incompetent without her mother. Ultimately this results in a struggle over separation during which the mother is angry that her daughter is growing up and the daughter is angry that her mother is so controlling and critical. This whole dynamic sets up body image problems because it's difficult for this girl to feel good about herself and know that her body is her own.

The Critical Mother: This is the mother who shows her anxiety in a different way; she's so anxious for her daughter to be popular and successful that she offers constant critiques and advice to "help" her daughter. She's got lists of dos and don'ts. If only, she thinks, her daughter would just *listen* to her, she'd be assured of success—all of which sets her daughter up for seeing any problem she encounters as a sign of failure and her own inadequacy. She reads all of her mother's critiques as a strong vote of no confidence. She feels unable to please her mother and thus becomes unsure of herself.

The Critical Mother acts the way she does because of her own low self-esteem and self-doubts. Having a daughter who's "perfect" helps her compensate for these feelings. She's frantically trying to keep up appearances and please others, and she insists that her daughter do the same.

The Critical Mother is the one who would say, "You never put enough effort into . . . ," or, "If you would try harder, you would be the best. But you obviously don't care." There are lots of *always* and *nevers* and *shoulds* and *shouldn'ts* in the speech patterns of this mother. She says, "What will people think?" With the whole world's eyes on her and the bar raised this high, how could her daughter *not* have body image problems?

One type of Critical Mother is the *Traditional Mother*, who is also worried about what people will think. For her life to function smoothly, everything has to be the way it always was, so she's completely unable to cope with a daughter who wants pink streaks in her hair or tattoos on her ankle. Her message to her daughter is "Be like me. If you're different, no one will ever love you." There's another subtle message here: "If you're different, *I* won't love you."

THE SUPER MOTHER

This is the mother who's not content to be just your regular Super Mom. She's a Type A-plus, an overfunctioning, perfectionistic overachiever. She's the one who brings homemade lasagna for twenty to the PTA meeting after she's worked all day. She looks at her daughter's typical adolescent behavior and angst as signs of weakness. She freaks out when she sees her daughter doing normal adolescent things like talking on the phone for hours when she should be doing her homework, or lying on the couch eating chips and watching *Dawson's Creek* reruns.

Even if she tries not to be judgmental, judgment comes through in everything she does or doesn't say. She is always communicating shame and blame; she is fault-finding, constantly correcting. She interprets her daughter's normally negative teenage behavior as something personal, intended to spite her. This is a mother who can't find common ground to communicate with her daughter, so she's constantly frustrated. Since she can't tolerate any failure in herself, she can't live with her daughter's adolescent imperfections, and so she distances herself from her daughter.

At fifteen, Megan is distressed; she's decided that her friends (although she loves them dearly) are boring, so she dyes her hair, paints her nails black, and gives away any item of clothing that is pink or pretty. She becomes irritable, overreactive, and generally is in a constant bad mood. Her mother asks her what's wrong:

MEGAN: You can't help me.

MOTHER: Then I've failed as your mother. If you can't talk to me, then I haven't done a good job in raising you.

MEGAN: You don't understand. I can't talk to you because you're suspicious of everything I do, everyone I'm with. If I tell you something is wrong and I feel bad, you make it seem like it's all my fault. All you want to do is figure out what I did wrong and blame me.

MOTHER: Well, you probably did do something wrong. You're far from perfect.

MEGAN (accusingly): You don't want to know about my feelings. You just want to blame me. And when I tell you that I feel bad, you say I shouldn't feel that way. So I give up.

In her need to be the perfect mother, the Super Mother is obsessed with her daughter's performance in all areas. When it comes to nutrition and health, being on a constant diet herself, she's vigilant in monitoring her daughter's weight and size. She makes comments like "You look like you've gained weight," or she'll ask, "You look better. Did you stop buying Coke and chips at school?" She's enormously invested in her daughter's romances, knows every score her daughter got on her PSATs and SATs, and helps her write her college essays. She's the mother who gets up at 5:00 A.M. to help her daughter memorize her calculus.

This mother finds it difficult to understand her daughter. Why *wouldn't* she want to take all honors courses, play varsity tennis, tutor underprivileged kids, and join the Future Leaders of America? If she just budgeted her time and stopped watching *Dawson's Creek*, she could do it all. The daughter of this mother feels that to win her mother's love, she has to pretend that she wants what her mother wants. She either gets with the program or she's out in the cold. There's no middle ground.

THE NOT ENOUGH MOTHER

This mother can't give her daughter what she needs emotionally. She's essentially missing in action. The reasons are often complex, but some common contributing factors are that her own mother was inadequate, that she doesn't understand her adolescent daughter's need for mothering, or that her own problems so overwhelm her that she can't meet her daughter's needs. This mother is typically underinvolved, either because she assumes her daughter is all grown up or because she finds other things in her life more gratifying than mothering.

The Not Enough Mother can't accept that she and her daughter aren't identical and is often threatened by her daughter's behavior; the result is that she is unable to establish a sympathetic connection with her daughter. The mother-daughter relationship is marked by power struggles which leave them both feeling alone and alienated. In the worst-case scenarios, the daughter develops severe body image issues from this lack of connection. She winds up having a "mother hunger" that is so extensive that she turns her anger and physical need for mothering inward, against her own body. This is the girl most likely to be promiscuous, less for sex than for physical contact and nurturing from boys and men. She will be vulnerable to various kinds of abuse, through drug use, alcohol, and unhealthy relationships.

Depression is a common characteristic of the Not Enough Mother. She doesn't have the energy, optimism, or wherewithal to develop or sustain a relationship with her daughter. In addition, she has difficulty relating to her daughter's concerns with body image because she's given up on her own. This mother, unable to give, pushes her daughter out of the nest too early. Paradoxically, she is so needy herself that she is unable to give her daughter the emotional foundation she will need to succeed.

The Not Enough Mother doesn't initiate heart-to-heart talks; she thinks if her daughter has something important to say, she'll speak up. It's easy for her to rationalize that nothing she has to say to her daughter will make any difference, since her daughter doesn't listen to her anyway. She takes what her daughter says at face value; it's also easy for her to believe her daughter's assertions that she's all grown up and doesn't need anything from her mother. She ignores evidence of problems, convincing herself that her daughter is just going through a stage that she will grow out of on her own. Such selective hearing gives this mother a false sense of security.

SUCCESSFUL MOTHERING requires that you look at yourself and be willing to examine your own ideas and behavior. Mothers find it easy to imagine that their daughters need to change; what they can't imagine is that *they* need to change. Yet one of the most valuable aspects of parenting an adolescent is that it compels you to reexamine and reconnect with yourself—with your own sexuality, relationships, friendships, and accomplishments. Use this time positively to meet your daughter's challenges by understanding yourself. See this time, if you can, as an opportunity to appreciate what you like about yourself and to change what you don't. Know that life and growth is all about change for you and your daughter. Be nourished and stimulated by all the new and evolving events in your daughter's life. Share in her growth and creativity. Tap into her intellectual energy. She'll grow and you will, too.

Chapter 7

HUSBANDS AND FATHERS

THE IRONY OF the father-daughter relationship is that just when a girl starts to have trouble connecting with her father and to feel that she has little in common with him, she actually needs him most. A father (if he can hang in there) can do amazing things for his adolescent daughter (if she'll let him). He can mentor, nurture, and protect her. And he can offer her a look at life from a masculine point of view. Who better to help her understand the opposite sex than someone of the opposite sex? Especially someone whom she can trust.

A father's acceptance, appreciation, and enjoyment of his daughter are central to her developing a healthy sense of herself and giving her the crucial affirmation that she needs to feel desirable as a female. In fathering, like everything else, success breeds success. When a father is close to his adolescent daughter, he will find ways to stay involved. This will help them both develop a mutually rewarding relationship in which normal parent-child tensions can be worked through, stress can be tolerated, and conflicts can be acknowledged and addressed. A father's relationship with his daughter is a process that parallels your own, but one that has its own pay-off for a girl's emotional and intellectual development. When a father gives his daughter his love, he makes her feel secure at an anxious time in her life. When he shares his knowledge of the world with her, he teaches her, mentors her, and encourages her to think for herself. And his seeing her as a whole person helps to strengthen her, helps her separate from her mother, and allows her to develop other healthy relationships and gain confidence.

In all these ways, a father's role is quite specific in its contribution to his daughter's growth. Their relationship is unique. Her father is the first person of the opposite sex whom she knows and loves. Her experience of feeling loved and valued by a man begins with her relationship with her father. Her intense love for him is a normal part of the Oedipal process. This (think back to Psych 101) is where a young girl "falls in love" with Daddy and starts separating from Mommy. A healthy love triangle forms between her, her father, and her mother. As part of this triangle, Mommy becomes a rival for the very special attention of Daddy. You may remember the time your young daughter turned to you and said, "I'm going to marry Daddy." Everyone laughed and you gently said, "Daddy's already married to Mommy. But someday you'll find someone just for you."

In the normal course of the Oedipal process, a girl is frustrated in her desire to have her father all for herself. Over time she gives up her rivalry with her mother and gives up her quest to be her father's true love. It's then that she turns back to her mother and deepens the healthy, ongoing process of identifying with her as a woman. And it's then that she can start to sort out the Oedipal triangle, put her relationship with her parents in perspective, and eventually achieve a real separation.

A natural result of the conflict your daughter goes through is that it draws you and your husband closer together. And when the two of you have a good relationship, there's a feeling of great safety for your daughter. She won't have the opportunity (both tantalizing and terrifying) to get rid of you and have Daddy all to herself. She'll be able to understand what a good relationship is like. Along with learning valuable lessons about love, she'll get a good sense of the boundaries of relationships, both in friendship and love. Everyone benefits when you and your husband can help raise your daughter together. When they mesh well, the different roles you play will go a long way toward easing the tensions that naturally arise from her quest to forge her own identity.

And what, you might ask, happens if you and her father *don't* raise your daughter together? Her interest in and need for her father will remain an important part of her development. And if her father—whether because of death, divorce, separation, or living in a nontraditional family—isn't available, she'll have issues to address. There are two ways you can help her. First, be sensitive to these issues. And second, provide her with a male figure who will be an active, involved, parental figure for her. Whether he's a good friend, stepfather, uncle, or grandfather doesn't really matter. What does matter is that you have given her a man to look up to and have an ongoing relationship with. These good-hearted men, by the way, the ones who possess the courage to step in and mentor a young girl, deserve a great deal of praise for taking on a tough job.

The need for a father doesn't go away. When your daughter reaches puberty, the Oedipal process takes on even greater meaning. Her need for attention from her father increases and intensifies. It's a confusing, conflicted kind of need because she herself is shy and confused; uncomfortable with her developing body, she alternately wants attention from her father and wants to push him away. She handles all this with varying degrees of success, depending on how available her father is and how supportive you are of her relationship with him. If these two pieces are in place, she'll thrive; she will be able to spend more time with her father, continue to share her world with him, and ultimately expand her relationship with him.

But when there's a disruption in your relationship or when one of you isn't there for her, problems are likely to arise. These problems can take a lot of different forms. It's possible that a girl will become so overwhelmed by her intense hunger for her father's affection that she'll pull away from him and start to cling more to you. Alternately, she may try harder to engage him by becoming the perfect daughter—mirroring his personality and taking his interests as her own. She may feel the only way to get close to him is by acting more like a son than a daughter. Conversely, she may fashion herself as

Daddy's Little Girl all over again, only this time in a more aggressive way: she'll wage war with you, try to drive a wedge between you and her father, and automatically take her father's side on everything.

So the big question is, if a daughter's need for her father is so acute, if the father-daughter relationship is so valuable, why is it so difficult to maintain? What makes it so hard for teenage girls and their fathers to get along? Most problems start when Daddy's Little Girl matures and stops being Daddy's Little Girl. Along with getting hips and zits, she starts to get an attitude. On the planet where the alien who has invaded your daughter's body lives, it's now an anti-Daddy world. Practically overnight, she stops being so sweet and loving to him and starts ignoring him, talking back to him, slamming doors, being disrespectful, recoiling from his touch, telling him he's stupid, keeping secrets from him, colluding with her mother and girlfriends against him, making fun of everything from how he dresses to what he's watching on TV. She's embarrassed to be seen with him. Her lifelong adoration has been replaced by contempt and disdain. He's become totally incapable of doing anything right. It's as if she's had an allergic reaction to him. He, of course, is stung and hurt, feeling rejected and not knowing why.

At this point many fathers conclude that their daughters don't need them. They feel shut out, helpless, unable to make a meaningful effort to be included. They see that their daughters, animated and engaged with the rest of the world, behave in just the opposite way with them. What they have no way of seeing is their daughters' continued need for fathering. It's not surprising that many fathers become resentful; they feel that they're just there to drive their daughters to the mall or to pay the bill for clothes no father would approve of.

What a father often doesn't understand is that his daughter is uncomfortable with him because she is so uncomfortable with herself. Her antagonism and attitude toward him comes from her discomfort and shyness. It's especially hard for him to see this because she seems so bold. With her changing body and her ambivalent feelings of desire for him, she rides a nonstop roller coaster of emotion. Besides her general negativity toward him, she acts out in other ways that come directly from her insecurity and immaturity about her sexuality. So she'll flirt with her father, she'll provoke him, she'll taunt him, she'll tease him. And her father, who has no context for any of this beyond the cliché that girls in adolescence are impossible, only sees that his daughter is acting out in inexplicably brazen ways. "You ruin everything," she tells him. "You don't understand that I'm grown-up now." "I'm wearing this whether you like it or not." It's as though the first thirteen years never existed.

No area is as much a minefield for a father to navigate as his daughter's maturing body. Her body image issues are now highly sexualized. She is continually testing him, looking for an affirmation of her sexuality and attractiveness. For adolescent girls with womanly bodies they don't quite know what to do with, life is like having a learner's permit and driving around in a Porsche.

The earlier, simpler role a father may have had—playing with his daughter or filling in for Mom—now feels irrelevant. His daughter makes it clear to him that he's no longer contributing anything valuable, and she doesn't help him find new ways to stay involved. When she does acknowledge his presence, she sees him as an authority figure, and that authority becomes the source of her rebellion.

If no one clues him in, the result is catastrophic. It's not a problem only for the father and daughter, but for you and your whole family as well. Just when you're trying to work out issues of your own with your daughter, you've got a ringside seat, whether you want it or not, for their volatile, ongoing love-hate battle. (And as bad as the volatility is, even worse is a frosty silence between them.) They quarrel, bait each other, trade criticisms, have screaming matches. Doors slam, threats are issued. Over-the-top punishments are handed out. He's caustic, she's sarcastic. She's provocative, he's punitive. She's defiant, he's self-righteous. She yells, he yells louder.

Finally, if it gets *really* bad, a father starts to give up on his daughter because the whole thing seems like a losing cause. He convinces himself that you, as her mother, understand her better than he does. His confusion, coupled with a need you may feel to stay closer to a daughter who seems newly vulnerable and volatile, can push him out the door. On his way out he's likely to blame either your daughter or you for what's happening, or at worst both, as if you'd been conspiring against him.

The daughter who rewarded him in the past and made him feel so good about himself now only makes him feel terrible, and he cannot tolerate either the loss or the failure. For her part, an adolescent girl does not begin to understand *his* behavior. Why is he so out of control? Why can't he see how much she needs him? Why doesn't he realize how much she is suffering? She's hurt by his withdrawal, stung by his criticism. He is profoundly disappointed in her and she feels that disappointment without his having to say a word. It appears to her that he has abandoned her forever, and his withdrawal is a psychological blow. Once a girl has successfully forced her father out of her life, she's left with an empty victory. She's gained a sense of power that she never really wanted and shouldn't have had in the first place.

So where does this leave them? Both father and daughter are hostile and suspicious. Neither trusts the other. They may make guarded attempts to patch things up, but the situation is so loaded that nothing really holds. The result is a relationship in tatters.

You (surprise!) are caught in the middle. Your husband tells you, "She's impossible. *You* deal with her." Your daughter tells you, "I *hate* Daddy. I'm never talking to him again." (This is often followed by, "How could you have married him?") Take heart. If you understand what's happening and why, you can help. Of course, you can't control everything. You can't make the conflict and tension go away; don't expect miracles. But you can probably do more than you think you can.

In fact, with the right knowledge and tools, you can help

your husband understand your daughter, and you can help your daughter understand her father. You can keep yourself from being caught in their crossfire. You can look at how *you* might be making things harder for both of them. You can make sure you don't devote your life to being the family social worker or referee. You can keep your relationship with your daughter on an even keel and your marriage intact. And you'll be able to start to make sense of the father-daughter dynamic: their power struggles, her raging hormones, his confusion and hurt, her artful manipulations, his overreactions, and the staggeringly infantile behavior on both sides.

First of all, you can help your husband understand the basic dynamics of adolescence and fatherhood. He needs to know how insecure adolescent daughters really are and how much they have to deal with. An adolescent girl is the poster child for *issues*. By the time she reaches puberty and the Oedipal process kicks back in, she already has body image, sexuality, and identity issues in addition to all her other issues (popularity, grades, clothes, etc.). She is seriously *over*-issued. Now she has father issues, too. She is constantly aware of her father, self-consciously checking to see what he thinks of how she looks and what she is wearing and, whether she shows it or not, taking to heart all the comments he makes.

If, for example, he volunteers, "My daughter has the most beautiful smile," and glows with pleasure as he says it, he will have made his daughter's day. It's not just what he says, it's that he *volunteered* it that's so great. An adolescent girl doesn't want to *ask* to be admired, to have to fish for compliments or draw attention to her body. She needs to have her father come up with praise on his own. If what he says isn't what she wants to hear, she'll reject it outright or unconsciously. Of course, even if it *is* what she wants to hear, she may, out of insecurity and shyness, reject it or criticize him. (And you think it's hard to be her *mother*.) But no matter what, she is always tuned in to him: wanting to know his opinion, trying to gauge his sense of right and wrong, seeing where his sense of boundaries are between the sexes (especially between her and boys), wanting to see how concerned he is about her and how determined to protect her.

As much as she may want to trust him, even the most adoring daughter is now likely to be suspicious of her father's motives. She may think he doesn't really want any other man to pay attention to her. She'll say something like "Well, of course you hate what I'm wearing. You want me to look like some geeky loser, so no boy will look twice at me." She thinks the reason he doesn't like something she's wearing is that he's too conservative or controlling. She thinks he doesn't understand that things have changed since he grew up back in the Dark Ages. Does she have any idea of how sexy she looks as she says this? Probably not. After a father makes sure that the palpitations in his heart when he sees his little girl in skintight see-through sparkled spandex aren't a life-threatening cardiac episode, he needs to catch his breath and try to rise to the occasion. His goal is to handle these situations with something resembling maturity and grace.

If he resists offering his opinions about what she's wearing and gives her feedback only when she asks for it, his guidance can help. He needs to be particularly tuned in to her, since she may not even ask him directly. Of course, it helps to set some fashion limits before your daughter comes home wearing something eye-popping. It would be ideal to have guidelines about appropriate dress already in place the first moment your daughter looks outside the junior miss department and notices what Hollywood actresses are wearing. But what if you don't.

STACY: Daddy, how do you like my new outfit?
FATHER: If you want my honest opinion, it will get you
     noticed, but I think it's way too revealing. You're too
     pretty to dress like that. You want people to notice you,
     not what you're wearing.

Is it simple? No. With fathers and adolescent daughters, messages are often mixed and issues are seldom clear. While a daughter may be bold enough to wear something very sexy, she is often embarrassed to talk about her body or about any aspect of sex, especially with her father. And while one father worries that his daughter looks so sexy and voluptuous, another may find himself worrying that his daughter isn't sexually precocious or that she isn't trying to be flirty and feminine. He worries if she is overweight, if she's wearing sweatshirts and baggy sweatpants instead of micro miniskirts. All he can find to say is, "Why can't you wear a dress for a change? I don't know why you don't want to lose some weight or put on some makeup. No wonder you don't ever have a boyfriend."

Why is he saying this? A father looks at his daughter's appearance from his perspective as a man. He wants her to look attractive because he sees attractiveness as an indication of happiness and success. If a girl's looks go to one extreme or another, her father may get so anxious that he'll make inappropriate, controlling remarks. He may feel so threatened and uncomfortable, so unsure of what to say, that he responds with disdain, criticism, and sarcasm. He becomes so reactive to her body that he gets pulled into saying all the wrong things. He comments on her weight, her breast development, her fashion sense, her role models. "And just who do you think you are," he asks, "Jennifer Lopez?" Mistakenly turning body issues into self-respect issues, he announces that the way she dresses means that she's being disrespectful of her mother. He characterizes her friends with the same kind of ridicule. It's hard for his daughter not to feel that something (everything?) is wrong with her.

Some fathers deal with the issue very differently. A father may act as if he hasn't noticed that his daughter's body is developing. He truly believes that he is helping her by not noticing. (Can you say *denial?*) So he winds up never commenting, complimenting, or admiring her, taking the tack that it's better to say nothing than to say something wrong.

Then there's the father who, beyond ignoring his daughter's developing body, finds it easier just to skip over the girl part and treat her like a boy. (Can you say *clueless?*) To this father, treating her like a son is the highest compliment he can give her, when in fact it totally negates his daughter's femininity. Worse yet, he thinks it allows him to discuss her body and that of other girls, movie stars, and female athletes as though she were "just one of the boys."

The father who treats his daughter like a little princess—who buys her cute little outfits and loves when she acts seductive and flirts with him—unwittingly overstimulates his daughter and teaches her a terribly misguided lesson about sexuality. She may learn that her sexuality has great power, but she may never learn to trust men and their intentions. This is the same dad who will get too familiar with his daughter's friends and think it's okay to act like an adolescent boy himself. He rationalizes that he's "mentoring" when what he's really doing is flirting.

When a girl ignores her father and starts pushing him away, he is likely to wind up feeling hurt, angry, and resentful. But when a father ignores his daughter, puts her down, or treats her inappropriately, the consequences are far more devastating. Feeling that she's lost her father and not knowing why, a girl may try to manipulate her looks to please her father and revive his interest. This could mean anything from dyeing her hair in multicolored stripes to getting into an "If only I were thin . . ." mentality. She may start dressing very seductively in an attempt to get his attention through her sexuality. Or she may give up on him entirely and remain angry with her father without telling him. As a consequence of having such an unhappy relationship with him, she may give up on *herself*. She'll cover up her body and comfort herself with food. This is a girl who can easily develop strong feelings of self-loathing about her femininity. Unable to control her father's responses, she identifies with his rejection and rejects herself.

The girl who hears nothing from her father starts to feel like nothing. If her father doesn't say she's pretty, well, she figures, he must know. Or she may conclude that her father doesn't want her to grow up, that she is desirable to him only if she remains an undeveloped girl. This can easily set the foundation for an eating disorder, in which a girl views her developing body as the enemy. In Oedipal terms, she thinks her body must be the reason she has lost her father. Then, as she becomes insecure about his feelings for her, her rivalry with her mother for his attention intensifies.

Then there's the girl who isn't sure whether she's her father's daughter or his girlfriend. She may become adept at manipulating her father and the boys in her life, but in the future she will rarely enjoy genuinely good relationships with men.

On the other hand, an emotionally immature girl who is unaware of the impact of her sexuality may become inhibited and ashamed of her body because of her father's insensitive comments.

The girl whose father can't handle his daughter's sexuality and constantly disparages how she looks *does* achieve the safe distance she needs between herself and her father, but at the cost of devastating consequences for her self-esteem:

TONYA *(wearing the mini-est of miniskirts and what looks like Barbie's T-shirt):* Daddy, do you like my new outfit?

FATHER *(eyes popping):* You're going out looking like *that?* And just what do you think guys are going to think of you? No daughter of *mine* is going out like *that.*

In three sentences he manages to diminish and cheapen his daughter's sexuality, at the same time strongly suggesting that her sexuality is a bad thing. His self-consciousness lets him down, and of course his daughter has no way of knowing it's his issue, not hers. It doesn't take much to make an adolescent girl feel awful about her body, and conversely, it doesn't take much to make her feel a lot better. A father who says something appreciative or positive is helping his daughter. And when he doesn't make his comment sound like some edict—acknowledging that it's just his opinion—he's much more human and sympathetic to her.

Mothers bring their own issues and biases to the already fraught-with-problems father-daughter relationship. They can contribute to fathers' feeling marginalized. Typically, while their daughters are pushing them away for one reason, their wives are pushing them away for another. Mothers of adolescent daughters often put their husbands down as being clueless or dense. They think their husbands don't understand things as well as mothers do, that they don't share the same feelings or sensitivities, that basically they don't know what they are doing. They blame the men for not doing the right thing without telling them what the right thing is. And they start to distrust them, especially in the delicate area of parenting daughters.

Fathers *are* often awkward and unsure with their adolescent daughters, behaving in all the ways that embarrass them or make them uncomfortable. If this happens in your house, your daughter *is* likely to move away from her father and come running to you for protection. While her choice may be flattering, it also puts you right in the middle of the conflict. He can't deal with her. She can't communicate with him. And you start to believe that it's too risky to allow your husband to have a meaningful role in parenting. Since you don't know how to fix their relationship, it's easier to think that her father should keep his role of provider but hand over the parenting to you.

Your daughter (who will probably figure out what's happening before you do) may deepen the split by asking you why you married such a creep in the first place. Or she may say, "If you want to divorce Daddy, go right ahead, don't worry about me." She may even bait you: "You won't let me go to the party because you have to do what Daddy says. Why don't you have a mind of your own?" Your husband, not surprisingly, will resent both you and your daughter. He'll either retreat to his office, start taking his golf game a lot more seriously, or try to break into your tight mother-daughter duo, all of which will only lead to more fractured parenting for your daughter and more tension for all of you. The more your husband criticizes your daughter, the more you feel you need to defend her. The more conservative he is with her, the more permissive you are. Power struggles, adolescent acting out, and two parents who are on two different pages, giving her two different messages, are the unhappy result.

If you find yourself in this position, how can you get out of it? First of all, treat her father as a concerned parent, not as a potentially dangerous source of embarrassment. You have to turn to him as the other adult and make space for him in the family circle. Even divorced or unmarried parents can establish this family circle when they understand how vital it is for their daughter's growth. Fathers often fall into a power struggle when they feel they've been marginalized and devalued. They only get out of it when they're respected and given a real role to play in the family. If you roll your eyes and smile conspiratorially at your daughter when your husband says something stupid, you are not helping. Nor are you helping if you just let him get away with doing or saying something stupid. If, for example, your husband is yelling at your daughter about something—such as breaking curfew or cutting class—you might point out to him that he's got the facts and the argument right but not the way of presenting them. Explain that the louder he yells, the less she hears him.

Once you know that your daughter behaves the way she does with her father because she is unsure of herself, scared of her sexuality, and testing him, you can tell him so without appointing yourself her public defender. Then he can start, on his own, to improve his relationship with her. You can help with this without getting in the way. Fathers can easily fall into the role of the "good time" guy, the one who fills in for you when you're not around. No one seriously expects him to parent your daughter except when you're away or there's no one else to pick her up late from a party. If you see that this is how the roles in your family break down, you can help by diversifying who does what, bringing your husband into the loop, sharing information with him, and letting him know that you're willing to give up some of your territory. Remember that he can be tuned in only if he is clued in.

Don't fall into the trap of making your husband the heavy, the one responsible for making all the decisions you're uncomfortable with. Avoid saying, "Talk to your father about borrowing the car," or, "Tell Daddy you need permission to go to the concert," or, "Ask Daddy when *he* thinks you should be home."

Think about how you feel about including and sharing responsibilities with your husband. Do you miss being the one who knows everything? Do you wish you could control everything? Do you feel that your husband's presence will make your daughter value you less? Ask yourself if you have a problem telling him things. For example, do you *not* tell him about your daughter's problems because you think they are your fault? Do you worry that he'll blame you?

You and your husband need to put your heads together and make sure he has a real role to play in your daughter's life—one that both of you feel comfortable with. As girls today learn more about sex roles, they're quick to notice that despite the progress being made on gender equality, often women are still taking care of others and men are still just taking care of themselves. The most highly evolved girl is still saturated with the message that success is based on pleasing others and being desirable. Men only have to think about pleasing themselves. The male prerogative is envied by girls, but if they try to adopt it themselves, people think that they're acting selfish or bitchy. Having her father genuinely involved in her life gives a girl an opportunity to learn that men can be equally caring and nurturing.

A father often needs to learn when and how to appreciate his daughter's growth and development. Encourage him, suggesting very specifically when, how, and where to say something. A woman whose husband always managed to say something inappropriate or mortifying to their fourteen-year-old daughter suggested that he couldn't get in any trouble if he would comment only about how she looked from the neck up. So he limited his remarks to "Nice earrings," "Pretty ponytail," and "You look good with eye shadow," until he got better at compliments. It worked.

Knowing how touchy and volatile the subject of sexuality is, make it clear to both your daughter and your husband that no topic of discussion in a family should be considered taboo. Your husband might begin by being candid and acknowledging his own embarrassment. If he can make himself be open without being pushy or nosy, your daughter is more likely to come to him with her questions and concerns. Relate, if you can remember one, some story from your own adolescence about something dopey your father said to you. (What woman doesn't have a few of these committed to memory?)

Help your husband understand that even if he's really upset about something your daughter is doing or wearing, he shouldn't abdicate and pass all responsibility off to you because he's uncomfortable. For example: "You better tell Susie to take off those hot pants" and "I don't want her going out dressed like that." You're not his spokeswoman. Let him talk to her.

Give your husband feedback, a sense of balance, and some perspective. Appreciate him for his honesty and candor, his sense of humor, his straightforward approach to issues. Be grateful that he can, occasionally, act as a buffer between you and your daughter.

Encourage him to take risks to improve his relationship with your daughter. She may have pushed him away before, but let him know that he should keep trying. Remind him that growing up is a process. Ask him to try to remember what it's like to be a teenager. Tell him that if he takes a risk and makes a mistake, he can always say to his daughter, "I'm sorry I said the wrong thing," or, "I'm sorry I hurt your feelings." If he checks his intentions, evaluates what he said, and discusses it with her without demeaning or trivializing her feelings—"Why are you so sensitive?" "What are you getting so worked up about?" "I didn't mean it." "Can't you take a joke?"—she'll be more open to him.

Get your husband in the loop. Nothing is more discouraging than being the last to know. Ask yourself, are there times you don't want him to know at all? Do you love being your daughter's confidante so much that you want to keep secrets?

If your daughter gets her period, for example, it's okay to agree not to tell Daddy. But you should tell *her* that her father already knows about this stuff. Let her know that sooner or later, when the time is right, the two of you need to tell him. Don't act like you and your daughter are in some sort of girls-only club.

Give your daughter's father a reality check: he's not wrong, teenagers (and many preteens) *are* very sexy. And so are their friends. Hopefully he'll be smart enough not to act like a man with a midlife crisis. Having a real role to play as the adult male in his daughter's life helps a man behave responsibly. (This is the "rise to the occasion" part.) His genuine participation in parenting requires him to think about his daughter's real needs, so that he's not just looking at her appearance but helping her develop on the inside.

In an ideal family situation (is that an oxymoron?), your husband will encourage your daughter's identification with you. He'll say something like "You and your mother are the only people I know who start crying at the opening credits of the movie." Or, "You got your good sense of humor from your mom." Explain to your husband that this makes your daughter's relationship with him safer; she knows she's not replacing you. Her father loves the two of you separately and appropriately.

The role a father plays is not always well defined, it's rarely easy, and it's often unsung. But while he may not be directly involved in his daughter's body-related issues, his empathy and positive feedback will encourage her to value herself.

Feeling loved by the first man in her life lets her hold her head high and feel a sense of dignity. Her father proves to her that men aren't mysterious. He answers for her the question that every woman will ask, sooner or later—will somebody really love me for myself? Yes, he says, every time he smiles when she walks in the room, every time he laughs at her jokes, every time he honestly tells her what he thinks about her appearance. When a girl has a sense of security in the love of her father, she is much more likely to find a love of her own.

WHAT NOT TO SAY OR DO
A LIST FOR YOUR HUSBAND

Don't criticize your daughter's diet or her figure; don't comment on her size or her style.

Don't flirt with or be adorable with her friends. And don't tell stupid jokes or try to insinuate yourself into their conversation.

Don't try to be cooler than the other dads. Don't say, "Sure you can have a keg party," or, "Want to smoke a joint?"

Don't try to be cooler than her mother. Don't say, "I would let you have a keg party, but you know your mother," or, "Want to smoke a joint? Wait until your mother leaves."

Don't be so controlling or overprotective that you make your daughter feel self-conscious or embarrassed. "Oh, that sweater is way too tight. Where do you think you're going dressed like that?"

Don't encourage her to wear clothes that are too sexy or sophisticated. Conversely, don't buy her sweats in XXL.

No matter what she's wearing when she walks into the room, avoid any sentence that starts with "Oh, my God" or "No daughter of mine . . ."

Don't be dismissive of her girliness. Don't act as if being a teenage girl is a condition of insanity. Don't comment on how chatty, silly, flighty, moody, shallow, or fickle she is.

Don't try to solve her boyfriend problems with wise male advice you got when you were fifteen. (Do try to remember her boyfriend's name.)

Don't try to be her friend. What she needs is an adult male in a fathering role.

Don't overreact to her criticism.

Don't be seduced by her, but don't assume she's always trying to manipulate you or manipulate all the money out of your pocket.

Don't ever put down women. Don't objectify them. Don't look at them as sexual objects. Don't be a breast man or a thigh man unless you are ordering a piece of chicken. Don't ogle the models in Victoria's Secret commercials.

WHAT TO DO

Admire women.

Let your daughter see you hug her mother once in a while. And if you're divorced, don't say disparaging things about her mother.

Pay attention to your daughter—to her ideas, problems, conflicts, opinions. Treat her seriously. Give her a sense that she's not a silly teenager but a person with valuable ideas and opinions. If she sounds illogical, help her figure out how to be more logical.

Teach her what a hat trick, a trifecta, a give-and-go, a Hail Mary Pass, and a Texas leaguer are.

Take her to a chick flick once in a while and don't make fun of it.

Admire her throwing arm and then admire her earrings.

Show up—at the play, at the game, at the dinner table. But stay out of her room.

Be there because you want to be, not because she begs you or her mother drafts you. Be part of her life even if she's not jumping up and down to thank you.

Reassure her that if she has guests over, you won't grill her boyfriend or spend hours asking her friends where they want to go to college.

Try to be accepting of her boyfriend, even if he looks kind of weird to you.

Chapter 8

TEENAGE GIRLS, THE CARE AND FEEDING OF

SOMEWHERE BETWEEN the refrigerator and the freezer, the kitchen and the dining room table, you and your teenage daughter are likely to get into some pretty intense discussions (okay, big fights) about what's on her plate. If you have a teenage daughter, you have a daughter who is likely to have some rather unusual and highly original ideas about food and nutrition. Chances are, from about the age of thirteen on, she will eat in ways that will make you crazy. She may go on diets that will appall you, come up with wildly misguided ideas about nutrition and exercise, and become obsessed with food, dieting, and weight, with calories and fat grams, with thin thighs and a flat stomach.

As she grapples with her body image issues, be prepared for the fact that your daughter will not eat a healthy diet. The FDA food pyramid and leafy greens will not be part of her vocabulary, although she will be scrutinizing the nutritional labels on packages. She will develop unhealthy attitudes to food. In the worst-case scenario, she will not *be* healthy. And if you think *that's* scary, what's *really* scary is knowing that she will be part of a large majority. Statistics show that teenage girls have the poorest nutrition of any age group in the United States today. Many are literally starving. Very few are eating the right foods or getting the right nutrients. So mothers who worry about whether their daughters are making smart decisions about boys and sex and drugs would do well to start worrying whether their daughters are making smart decisions about breakfast and junk foods.

And where do these girls get some of their most misguided nutrition ideas? Where do they pick up some of their worst eating habits? From their mothers. Their food-phobic, fat-obsessed, perpetually dieting mothers. The fact is that women today are at war with their bodies. If there is one thing you can do for your daughter, break the intergenerational cycle and help her make peace with her body. Otherwise, she'll be fighting it her whole life.

The good news is that you *can* make a difference. Of all the issues affecting your adolescent daughter, nutrition is one where (minor miracle) you actually have some control. Being uninvolved is not an option: helping your daughter improve her eating habits is part of a mother's job definition. And this is a time when you can express with food what you can't express to her directly. Because your daughter is doing so much to say, "Get out of my life," food can be the best way for you to keep an important connection. It's something your daughter still comes to you for.

The bad news is that you've got a hard job. Your daughter

doesn't care about being fit; she cares about not being fat. She doesn't care about what's best for her; she cares about fitting in and looking right. She doesn't care about her health; she cares about her shape. In her world, food has morphed into something that no longer has to do with sustenance or real hunger. It seems more like a bad habit, a weakness, an unfortunate requirement of life. Some foods are "good," some "bad." Some days she's "good" about what she eats, some days she's "bad." By the time a girl is an adolescent (and usually long before), food has gotten so disconnected from its real meaning and value that eating is a negative experience. She disconnects food from pleasure and food from fuel. To an adolescent girl, food = fat. Fat = the enemy.

Because she feels that so much of her life is out of her control, she may attempt to use food to feel successful and in control. But when she tries, especially through dieting, she often sets up unrealistic goals and impossible expectations. "I'm only going to eat five hundred calories a day," says the girl who wants to lose five pounds in five days. "It's so hard for me to lose weight because I have a slow metabolism," says the constantly fasting girl who has no idea what a metabolic rate is and who doesn't understand that what she's doing can actually affect the rate of her metabolism in a negative way. It doesn't take long for these girls to experience diets as disastrous and their bodies as a source of stress and failure. They get so hungry that they eat impulsively and then hate themselves. Then the only thing that gets lowered in these extreme low-calorie diets is their sense of self-esteem.

If food isn't nourishment or pleasure or fuel or sharing or a way of connecting, then exactly what *is* it for an adolescent girl?

FOOD IS A POWER STRUGGLE.

You may make a nutritious meal, only to have your daughter refuse to eat any of it. Or you'll go out of your way to buy special food, something you know she loves, only to have her announce that she hates it. You don't even have to *see* your daughter to fight with her about food. Girls today are often on their own when it comes to eating. Aside from being at school all day, many of them spend most of their time at home in their own rooms. One of the consequences is that the social aspects of sharing a meal together become separated from eating. The girls who are most resistant to sitting down at the family dinner table are the ones who are trying to stay on rigorous diets. They want total control over what they're eating, and family meals present too many temptations.

Another consequence of your daughter's increasing independence is that you don't really know (except by the wrappers, empty soda cans, and decaying food in her backpack) what she is eating. The lack of structured meals, the isolated eating, and the all-day grazing compromise nutrition and reinforce disordered eating behaviors.

FOOD IS THE ENEMY.

"I don't eat that anymore," your daughter will say. "It's really bad for me." (*Carrots* are bad for her? *Casseroles* are bad for her?) Or she'll get enraged with you for preparing something that you *know* will make her gain weight. "Do you know how many calories are in that chicken pot pie?"

"Don't tell me what to eat; I'll get my own dinner," snaps the teen charm queen. "Gross," she announces to her mother, "that's dripping with butter. I can't eat that." When she's that difficult and argumentative, she often succeeds at pushing her mother away. That's when the problem starts. Her mother drops out, leaving her daughter to make decisions about what she eats on her own. But an adolescent girl is likely to make an uninformed decision, since she often sees food only as something that can make her fat. Even if she's more mature, she may not have the interest or patience to put together the nutritional balance her body needs.

FOOD WORKS MAGICALLY.

An adolescent girl will say something like "You're serving meat *and* potatoes? Everybody knows you should never have protein and carbs together. The carbs turn to fat immediately. It's a chemical reaction." If you ask her how she knows, she'll say, "*Everybody* knows that."

FOOD IS A LANGUAGE
EVERYONE SPEAKS BUT YOU.

Adolescent girls talk to each other a lot about their war with food, about the fat grams in a peanut butter cracker or the calories in a muffin. They tell each other what they've eaten; they comment on it; they monitor their choices and make value judgments on them. What they are really doing when they communicate in this way is using their friends as mother substitutes. In their war with food, girls impose stringent demands on themselves; then, not having the internal control or self-discipline to follow through on their own, they place their friends in the kind of overseer role their mother used to have. One girl will say to another, "How could you let me eat that?" or, "Why didn't you stop me from having that last piece of pizza?" Their constant focus on food and weight and their scrutinizing of each other's choices mirror the way they hear their mothers talk to *their* women friends about *their* diets. Food, for this new generation of self-critical eaters, has come to equal value judgment and anxiety.

FOOD IS SECRET.

Sometimes girls don't talk about it at all. When their war with food intensifies and they are on their way from disordered eating to a full-blown eating disorder, they start to be secretive about food. They binge late at night. They obsess about food twenty-four hours a day and say, "None for me, I'm not hungry," when they're famished. They lie to their mothers and to themselves about how much they've eaten or how much weight they've lost. They pretend everything is normal when it's anything but that.

FOOD IS EMBARRASSING.

To an adolescent girl, food says a lot about her. From what and how much she chooses (Does she look piggy?) to how she eats (Will she spill something because she's nervous? Is she chowing down like a truck driver?) to how it affects her image (Does she come off as unsexy? Uncool?). Many girls are so embarrassed and uncomfortable that they won't eat in front of boys at school and wind up not eating all day. Some girls can eat in front of boys but not with boys they really like. The equation? Boys have to be impressed. Food is embarrassing. So boys and food don't mix.

FOOD IS COMPETITIVE.

Girls don't want other girls to see them eating; they're too worried about being judged. Are they eating too much? Are their friends thinking they're too fat to have that cookie? Diets, on the other hand, are understood to make a girl look better or feel special. Diets can get the right kind of attention and inspire envy. "What diet are you on?" one admiring girl asks another. "How long have you been on it?" "How much have you lost?" "How long has it been since you've had anything with sugar in it?" Problems start when a girl is unable to maintain these kinds of unrealistic and unhealthy goals. If she cheats on her diet and gains weight, she's likely to be consumed by anger at herself. She sees herself as weak, not in control, and certainly not as good as others. Who, she thinks, could admire her? And out of this desperate need to maintain rigid control and be the perfect dieter can come an eating disorder.

FOOD IS SCARY.

If girls are worried about being fat, cheeseburgers are scary and chocolate chocolate chip ice cream is totally frightening. But guess what nutritionists say is most scary to teenage girls. A sandwich. The thought of eating that much bread, not to mention something fattening in between the slices, along with maybe butter and mayo and bacon, is too much to even think about. Of course, on a day when they feel *really* fat, lettuce can be scary. In their fear, many girls become midnight refrigerator raiders, eating furtively and secretly.

FOOD IS A FEELING THAT DOESN'T FEEL GOOD.

The chronically unbalanced eating habits of teenage girls—fad dieting, living on snacks from the vending machine, eating just one meal a day, surviving on a bag of potato chips—induce all kinds of abnormal body sensations. When they *do* eat something, even a little something, they feel full, and they dread this sensation. They've lost the sense of feeling good when they are full; they've lost the ability to recognize what it feels like to be hungry. Feeling empty makes them feel successful and sharper. And feeling full, to their way of thinking, is nothing to be proud of anyway; it's a sign of weakness. "I ate like a pig," a girl will say. "Now I feel sick." It follows that elimination functions are disturbed, too. These girls get constipated or bloated and don't know that it's because of their poor eating habits. They are creating a vicious cycle with their bodies. They think of eating as something that creates bad body sensations, something they want to avoid. They conclude, "I just feel better when I don't eat."

FOOD IS SOMETHING SOMEONE ELSE SHOULD WORRY ABOUT.

If girls do know something about good nutrition, they dismiss it entirely or often give the typical teenage response: "I know it but it doesn't apply to me." For most, any long-range consequences of poor diet are impossible to fathom. They'd rather be thin now than worry about brittle bones years from now. Short-range consequences of a poor diet, such as insomnia or irritability or concentration problems, are also dismissed as irrelevant or ascribed to other sources—anything to keep from admitting that they need more food.

For girls with actual weight problems, distorted thinking becomes even more problematical. They imagine that eating one cookie will do as much damage as eating the whole bag, and since they can't resist one, they do eat the whole bag. They make bargains with themselves, bargains that are impossible to keep. "I'll eat this now, then I'll starve myself later." Later they make the same bargain all over again. Suddenly they're wearing stretch jeans and sweats, attempting to hide from themselves the consequences of overeating. They feel helpless and full of shame. Despairing, they give up and eat more, deepening their disordered eating.

YOUR ROLE

If you assume distorted thinking about food is only your daughter's problem, think again. Food can be just as negatively charged for you. Food can be a form of control, a reward, a crutch. It can be a way for you to break your connection with your daughter. When food issues have devolved into pointless power struggles, a mother may choose to abdicate the care and feeding of her daughter. This leads to many different types of guilty rationalizations. A mother may talk herself into believing that her daughter is so independent that she knows what she's doing and doesn't need any help. It's a kind of "My kid is so smart and grown-up for her age" conceit. An insecure mother, one who is scared to take responsibility for nutrition and who wants to avoid any blame, may find it easier just to put her daughter in charge of her own food choices. A mother who wants to get back to her career or just get her life back may suddenly become too busy to do the food shopping and meal planning.

There are mothers who just don't relate to food themselves and have a hard time perceiving the need to provide. If they see the whole shopping-cooking-serving thing as a burden or a nuisance, they'll rely on takeout or fast food. These mothers will say, "I'm a lousy cook," or, "I'm a wonderful cook, they just don't like what I make." Such a mother has lost or never had a pleasurable connection with food, so in her family, food is something everyone eats quickly and no one savors.

There are mothers who don't take their daughters seriously. They hear them talking about some ridiculous diet or unrealistic exercise plan and treat these girls as if they are ridiculous, too. They may laugh at what's in the diet or make fun of their daughters for even considering it. Humiliation, not help, is all they can offer.

Some mothers have their own very real problems with food. A mother with lifelong weight problems is often scared that her daughter will be heavy, too. This mother thinks that weight problems are contagious. She's unclear about what's genetic and what's a lifestyle factor. Her fear and confusion can lead to a lot of distorted and damaging messages. This is the mother who puts her daughter on a diet from babyhood. She's the mother who will micromanage, restrict, monitor, and make food pronouncements for her toddler. "Oh, white sugar is so bad for Amy. Occasionally we give her organic honey." This is also the mother who attempts nutritional perfection for her young daughter. "We don't keep any cookies or cake in the house. Amy prefers fresh fruit." A mother who struggles with her own body issues has the potential to imbue every bite her adolescent daughter takes with guilt and moral judgments. By trying to give her a perfect model for healthy eating, she may set up so many forbidden food zones that her daughter feels driven to rebel. Look for her daughter in the Twinkie and Devil Dog aisle.

Some mothers cause problems by sending mixed messages. They expect their daughters to see food as vital and pleasurable in spite of the fact that they obviously don't see it that way for themselves. They can be oblivious to their daughters' concerns and unsympathetic to their fears. If they think back to when they were young and had the metabolism to eat just about anything, they may envy their daughters. Or they may think that since their daughters have beautiful figures, the girls have no right to be so worried about food. Such a mother says, "Oh, don't be ridiculous; go ahead and have the chocolate pudding."

If you're wrestling with your own food issues, try not to inflict them on your daughter or let them distract you from helping her. An important part of helping her grow up and become self-sufficient is teaching her to take care of her body and her health. Although she's no longer a baby and you don't have to feed her every meal, you do need to talk to her about what she needs nutritionally and listen to what she wants as a positive image of herself.

A lot of adolescent girls actually want their mothers to be more involved. They want their mothers to have responsibility for guiding their nutrition. Your daughter won't come out and say, "I really want you to be more involved with my diet."

But in truth, she doesn't know what to do. She's happy for you to guide her as long as you aren't controlling or intrusive and you avoid asking little kid questions: "So, what did you have for lunch today?" "Did you eat the whole apple? Why not?" "Well, did you at least drink the milk?" Again, it's a balancing act. At the same time that she depends on you for guidance, your daughter wants to (and deserves to) start making her own choices and have the sense that she has control.

While you are trying to find the right balance between leaving her alone and hovering over her every bite, be sensitive not just to her food issues but to her physical development. Adolescent girls naturally gain weight as they mature, usually around the ages of eleven to fourteen. Let your daughter know that she's *supposed* to gain this weight because of the estrogen her body is producing to get her ready for childbearing. Her breasts will get bigger and her hips will fill out. She will look rounder and more womanly. It's important to talk to her about what a girl's developing body does so that she doesn't panic that she's getting fat.

Unfortunately, if a girl goes into adolescence even a little overweight, she's likely to be thought of as a girl with a weight problem and stigmatized for it. No wonder such a girl is vulnerable to feeling that she's in a struggle with her developing female body. From early adolescence on, this girl looks at her body as her enemy; it reveals her weaknesses and betrays her. She doesn't trust that her developing body will be a source of strength and health; to her, *developing* is just a code word for looking and feeling fat.

Along with giving your daughter a crash course in Female Biology 101, you need to give her lessons in *how* to eat. The best way is by being a role model. It's not what you say to her, it's what you do. Sit down and eat with her. If you actually select and eat healthy foods for yourself, your daughter will get the right message. But if you're picking at your salad ("No croutons, no avocado, no cheese, fat-free dressing—on the side") and complaining about how you'd *kill* for the bacon cheeseburger with fries, your daughter will understand that salads are God's way of making women suffer. If your freezer is filled with Lean Cuisine and your refrigerator with diet soda and Finnish mineral water, how could your daughter not think that sugar and fat are the enemy? On the other hand, if you're eating well and exercising, some part of your daughter's consciousness will pick that up, too.

But what if you're saying and doing all the right things? What if your daughter is underweight or overweight and doesn't seem to care? Know that she probably cares very much but isn't buying into your sensible nutrition ideas or your offer to help because she's angry at her body. Overeating and extreme dieting are often signs of depression. Your daughter may be struggling with identity issues; she may not have the friends she wants; she may have felt unfairly criticized by you or her father. She may have given up and turned to food as comfort, as sanctuary, or as protest against the demand to be pretty, pleasing, and perfect. The girl who overeats is treating her body like a barrier; it's something that can protect her. The extreme dieter sees fat as failure. She feels successful only when she's cutting back on her calories, no matter what the cost. That cost can become an eating disorder.

If the real goal of the nutritional messages you give your daughter is that you want her to look good, she will pick that up immediately. If your focus is on her attaining popularity through a good figure, chances are she'll protest through her body. She'll act out with food and gain weight, defeating you and herself in the process. So if your daughter is constantly struggling with her weight and her emotions, look at the possibility that something deeper is going on. Her unspoken message to you is "You can't control me," followed by "I'm grown up enough to lose control." And who will your angry, unhappy daughter blame for her loss of control? You and herself.

Some mothers are puzzled by their daughters' eating habits but don't think about digging deeper. Others worry that if they say something—*anything*—about what their daughters are eating, the girls will take the comment as controlling and critical and be defensive. Mothers worry that if they say enough of the wrong things, they will inadvertently *trigger* an eating disorder. Be reassured: you can say a thousand naggy things and not trigger an eating disorder. Your daughter could go on a different diet every week and *that* wouldn't trigger an eating disorder either.

There is a big difference between *disordered eating* and an *eating disorder*. Disordered eating is more or less the teenage norm. Like many things in adolescence, it's random, extreme, and impulsive. Remember that eating is *the* vulnerable area for girls. The brightest, most sensible and centered adolescent girl—one who can cope with everything from her parents' divorce to a major move smack in the middle of tenth grade—will burst into tears if she sees an inch of cellulite on her thighs.

How to spot disordered eating? Your daughter goes on a grapefruit-only diet for two days, then goes out for pepperoni pizza and onion rings with her friends. She refuses to eat anything but spaghetti and tomato sauce for dinner for weeks on end. She won't have eaten a vegetable for months, then she'll be a strict vegetarian for two months, then she'll get a hot dog at the ball game.

An eating disorder is something different. It has a huge underlying emotional component. Food and calories are rigidly restricted (anorexia), or food is eaten and then thrown up (bulimia), or there's a combination of restricted eating and bingeing. The causes of an eating disorder are far more complex than a nagging mother or a series of diets. To get a clear (and heartbreaking) look at one mother's story about an eating disorder, along with some real world tips, go to Andreasvoice.org online or read one of the books in the Resources section.

Here are specific ways you can help:

- Make sure that when you do make a comment, what you say is about your daughter's nutrition or health, not her weight.
- Don't talk about food being "good" if it's no-fat or "bad" if it's fattening. Carrots aren't "good" and cake isn't "bad." (Carrot cake, of course, is always very good.)
- Shame shouldn't be part of eating. ("I hate myself for eating the whole cake.")

145

- Don't talk about food issues with your daughter while you're eating.
- Don't disparage her friends and their food and diet advice. Don't say, "Well, that sounds stupid," even if it does.
- Keep in mind that with food, like everything else, adolescents tend to have black-and-white thinking. Explain to your daughter that it's not all or nothing. If, for example, she agrees to start having breakfast, reassure her that a "good breakfast" doesn't have to be a 2,000-calorie orange juice, fried eggs, bacon, and home fries extravaganza.
- Adolescents are easily impressed with what their friends say, and little ideas can become big truths. If some food advice or diet wisdom is passed on to them by a friend, it's seen as The Gospel According to Jennifer. Gently suggest that your daughter get a second opinion.
- Little ideas can also become a big thing if *you* choose to blow them out of proportion and fight about them. ("If you don't have milk every day, you're going to be three foot two and hunched over like a pretzel by the time you're my age.")
- Be realistic. If she's overweight, just signing her up with Jenny Craig and then expecting her to do it on her own is not a solution.
- If your daughter asks for help, create a more successful strategy than the fad diets she's been on. Work with her. Ask, "How is this going to work?" "How can we make this work?" "How can I help in this?" "How involved do you want me to be?"
- Don't sit around self-righteously nibbling on raw vege-

tables, insisting that you never want to dig into a pint of Chunky Monkey. Admit you're human. Eat a sandwich now and then. Have some potato chips and a brownie. Let your daughter see that there are no forbidden foods and that you can have what you want, if you indulge in moderation. It is possible to have a small piece of chocolate cake.

- Remember that food is and should be a pleasure. Go out for dinner. Don't count calories. Talk about how good it tastes. Enjoy yourself.

- Rent some movies that remind you and your daughter how satisfying and sensuous food can be: *Babette's Feast, Eat Drink Man Woman, Like Water for Chocolate.*

- Be more real about your own issues. Tell your daughter the truth—that you wish you weren't so hung up on how much you weigh; that you are trying to be less punitive with yourself for what you eat; that you're sorry if you act like the nutrition police with her.

Let your daughter know what she needs in her diet and help her get it. We're not talking about what might be nice for her to have in a perfect world. We're talking about what she *needs* today and every day to be healthy and strong and growing physically and mentally. What she needs so her hair will shine; so she can run a mile without stopping to catch her breath; so she can stay awake during first-period Calculus; so she can lug that fifty-pound backpack up and down the school stairs all day. And be realistic. The real world is hard: most girls are never going to eat five helpings of fruits and vegetables a day or drink three glasses of milk. They'd rather sleep late than get up for breakfast. They will often go weeks without eating anything green. Some are convinced that Froot Loops are a fruit. And a culture (an *overweight* culture, at that) that equates thinness with beauty and imbues it with an aura of moral superiority is sending them a toxic message that they can't entirely tune out. Do what you can to help your daughter feel good about her own body, help her be mindful about what she's putting in it, and don't leave that kitchen yet!

FEEDING AND NOURISHING YOUR DAUGHTER

Your daughter needs fat in her diet. Everyone does. Fat not only makes food taste good, it provides essential fatty acids and carries fat-soluble vitamins. Fat is also involved in the production of sex hormones; a certain amount of body fat is necessary to ensure menstruation, and eventually, a healthy and successful pregnancy. When girls lose weight and their body fat dips below a certain level, they stop getting their periods—a clear indication that things are not okay. The only way for your daughter to get the essential fatty acids her body needs is from fat in her diet. The bottom line is, you can't be healthy without eating some fat.

She needs to eat breakfast. Food eaten in the morning helps provide a kick-start to your daughter's metabolism. A healthy breakfast has some protein, some complex carbohydrates (whole grains and/or fruit), and a small amount of fat.

148

A poached egg on whole wheat toast and a glass of calcium-enriched orange juice are a good breakfast. So are melted cheese or peanut butter on a whole wheat English muffin and an orange, or a bowl of oatmeal with raisins and a glass of skim milk. A powdered doughnut and a 10 percent juice drink or a diet cola are not a good breakfast.

She needs some protein at breakfast. The body takes longer to process protein, so it will keep her feeling fuller longer and helps sustain her blood sugar level. Protein is wake-up food. Sugar is only a quick fix: it'll give her a quick surge of energy, and then she'll be back to feeling listless and hungry.

She needs to eat at semi-normal hours. Make sure your daughter isn't eating so late at night that it throws her whole metabolism out of whack. And watch her schedule: eating tends to get pushed back in the day. She'll skip breakfast, lunch is minimal, then afterschool activities get in the way, so she doesn't start eating until late in the day. By that time she's so hungry that her eating may be bingey. If she keeps snacking late into the night, she'll wake up not feeling hungry and the cycle will start all over again.

This, by the way, is the classic overeating pattern. This pattern affects insulin, which affects how the body stores calories as fat, which is partly why it can result in a girl being overweight. The way to break it is for your daughter to stop eating a few hours before bedtime; that way her body can rest during the night and she'll wake up hungry.

Let her in on what nutritionists know: eating late usually

has very little to do with hunger. People tend to eat at night because they are tired, not because they are hungry; they just can't tell the difference. And what they crave then late at night is carbohydrates, often in the form of sugary snacks. The answer when this happens? Don't eat. Take a nap instead, then wake up and do homework. Or go to bed early.

If you do only two things, a bit more protein and more regularly scheduled meals can make your daughter feel better almost immediately.

She needs something resembling a healthy diet. The key to a healthy diet, whether you're a teenager or not, is variety, balance, and moderation.

It's weird but true: if a girl eats *more* food *more* frequently, she'll actually weigh less. When she starts cutting back on her food intake, she signals her body to slow down its metabolism. That helps her avoid starvation, but it also slows down weight loss.

For millennia, food was scarce, so the human body evolved to cope with periods of famine. When food was scarce, the body automatically slowed down its metabolism to conserve fuel. Only recently have our bodies had to deal with an ongoing abundance of food. A New York nutritionist congratulates girls in her practice who come in because they are overweight. "Genetically," she tells them, "heavier people would have been the ones to survive."

Adolescent girls think that if they eat regularly, they will gain weight. The truth is that if your daughter eats regularly and more nutritiously, her body will find a healthy weight for her and stay there.

Balance and moderation at each meal, plus frequent eating, are the keys to keeping your daughter's metabolism at its most efficient level. She'll feel more energetic and she'll control her weight more easily.

She needs ten things every day: Calories (enough to give her energy). Protein (especially if she is vegetarian). Carbohydrates. Iron (15 milligrams a day if she is menstruating). Fat. Calcium (from milk, yogurt, cheese, fortified orange juice). Water. Lots of fruits and vegetables. A multivitamin. Exercise (an hour is ideal).

She needs to drink water. Your daughter needs about two and a half quarts of water a day. She doesn't have to drink it all directly; she can get some of it from eating foods like fruits and vegetables. Thirst isn't a good indicator of how much she needs to drink. People often confuse feelings of thirst with feelings of hunger, so they eat when they should be drinking water.

There's a simple way to know if your daughter is drinking enough water. (Tell her this is *not* a sneaky test for drugs!) If her urine is pale (like the color of lemonade), she is fine. If it's a deeper color (like apple juice), she is dehydrated.

Many girls are underhydrated because they don't like feeling bloated from fluid and they don't like having to go to the bathroom all the time. (Who wants to miss anything? Trips to the bathroom are for gossiping.)

She should take a multivitamin every day. Nutritionists go from saying "It couldn't hurt" to "It's essential." A multivitamin is like health insurance, especially for vegetarians and most especially vegans, who have a hard time getting vitamin B-12 in their food. Lots of adolescent and teenage girls are anemic, so the extra iron is important for them.

Ideally, your daughter should also take a calcium supplement (such as one of the chewable kinds), unless she always eats lots of dairy. Amy Peck, a nutritionist in Katonah, New York, says, "With multivitamins, a Chevy is as good as a Cadillac for the most part. A brand name like Centrum is good, but generic brands may be pretty similar and cheaper. Most companies buy their ingredients from the same few suppliers, so price is not necessarily an indication of a better choice." Kathy Levine, a Westchester, New York, nutritionist, says, "Try to get your daughter a multivitamin that approximates the RDA—one that has 100 percent of most things."

One problem with vitamins is that girls take them on an empty stomach, feel queasy, then don't want to take them at all. It's better to take vitamins with a snack after school or right after dinner. She shouldn't take vitamins with coffee; the acids can cancel out the nutrients.

What if your daughter is a vegetarian? Being a vegetarian makes it harder to get a nutritionally balanced diet, but it's not impossible. Vegetarianism, followed properly, is a great way to eat, but if your daughter is really a pizzaterian or a Cheez Doodleterian, look out. These girls tend to load on the fat and have anything but a balanced diet. Vegetarians who eat mainly pasta and cheese and butter and milk tend to put on weight. Normally girls don't go from having eating disorders to being vegetarian, but they do go from being vegetarian to having eating disorders. Vegetarianism can be one way to manage anxiety about weight and fat. It may also be the way your enlightened daughter chooses to express her views about politics, animal rights, and global health.

Don't immediately assume that your non-meat-eating daughter has an eating disorder. And don't be so concerned about respecting your daughter's politics that you sit back and let her pursue her vegetarianism without question. Make sure, no matter what, that your daughter reads a good book about the basics of a healthful vegetarian diet and that she understands how she has to eat to stay healthy.

If you suspect that your daughter may have an eating disorder in the guise of vegetarianism, get her to a doctor or nutritionist.

FREQUENTLY ASKED QUESTIONS

Q. What is "normal" eating? What is "normal" teenage girl eating?

A. Unfortunately, normal for teenage girls is skipped meals, unbalanced eating, too little protein, too many carbs, and too much diet soda. Ideally, however, normal eating means eating with enjoyment and paying attention to moderation and balance. Normal eating, at its most basic, is eating when you're hungry and stopping when you're satisfied.

Q. What's the difference between disordered eating and an eating disorder?

A. There is a *big* difference. *Disordered eating*, which is typical of teenage girls, means announcing that you only eat all-white foods (pasta, rice, etc.), then shifting into the "I'm so fat!" Frozfruit diet, then ordering a Big Mac and large fries without thinking twice. An *eating disorder* comes not out of random extremes of eating and dieting, but from a complex set of emotional components and a great deal of disordered thinking about food, fat, and what's in the mirror.

Q. When should I start to worry about her diet? Her weight? When should I get professional help from a nutritionist, pediatrician, or other doctor?

A. Certainly when she's too thin, putting on a lot of weight, or being evasive about what she's eating. But you might want to be more proactive and schedule the equivalent of a 15,000-mile tune-up for your daughter. When girls see a trip to a nutritionist as maintenance and not an occasion to be criticized, they're likely to have lots of good questions and be more open to discussing their concerns.

Q. What can I do if my daughter is seriously overweight and I think I need to do something whether she's asked me to or not?

A. Often, overweight girls are so sensitive about their diet that they reject help from their mothers. Broaden your network. Get some trusted friends involved, ones you know your daughter has a good relationship with. They can help you broach this ultrasensitive subject with your daughter. Find a doctor and a nutritionist who treat obesity in teens and can offer medical supervision for her weight loss. Resist your daughter's zealous suggestions of quick fixes, like buying some fat-burning exercise bike she saw advertised on TV. Develop a comprehensive plan that involves healthy weight loss, nutrition counseling, and exercise. Avoid all fad diets. Encourage her to find programs with peer support, like Weight Watchers. If your daughter wants to go to a weight-loss center or camp, make sure her goals are realistic and that she continues with a maintenance program when she gets back. Never bribe, never embarrass, always empathize, never micromanage. Be sure to keep nutritious food in your house.

Q. What about just calling a nutritionist or pediatrician with a question?

A. Ask about scheduling only a few visits. Ask about whether a nutritionist would be okay with preventive or maintenance work, just to keep your daughter within healthy boundaries. Establish a relationship, then call with any questions you or your daughter has.

Q. How can I help her deal with peer pressure? How can I compete with her friends at school who say, "You look so great thin." "Wow, you've lost weight. You look fabulous."

A. We live in a culture of thinness. If you talk to her about it—

ask her questions about what's healthy, how she feels physically, what she thinks is best for her—you can add a rational voice to the mix. Give her a sense of being able to figure it out so she's got more than the information that's coming from her friends. And be real: a concave stomach is something all girls want; you can't persuade her that she doesn't. (An adjunct to peer pressure is helping your daughter help a friend whom she suspects might have an eating disorder. She needs to know that this is one of those times when the problem might be so serious that she could violate a confidence and alert a parent or teacher.) One of the things you need to ask yourself is *how* your daughter has lost weight. Is she doing something unhealthy to look thin? Is she throwing up in the bathroom or running 10 miles a day or doing hundreds of crunches a day? Examine your own values and the values at home. Look at what her father is thinking, what her brothers are saying. Is there an overemphasis on appearance? Are you all quick to judge on looks rather than on substance?

Q. Does dieting ever make sense?

A. Nutritionists all say that restrictive dieting and calorie counting doesn't work. Just the word *diet* is considered a mistake. If your daughter is overweight and she *does* want to take pounds off, help her change her approach to eating instead. One way is to add structure to her eating. People who gain weight are not in touch with their bodies; their eating is more about pleasure and emotional rewards.

Your daughter needs to eat regularly throughout the day and to plan what she eats so that food becomes less of a reward or an emotional Band-Aid.

If your daughter can avoid extremes of hunger or fullness, she will end up moderating her food intake without "dieting." Dieting is like holding your breath. Sooner or later you will gasp for air (or food) and end up taking in more than you would have if you hadn't restricted yourself so severely. The answer is for your daughter to eat smaller amounts of food every three or four hours. If she doesn't get ravenously hungry, she won't overeat trying to catch up.

Q. What are the psychological effects of dieting?

A. The result of self-imposed food deprivation is a chronic obsession with food. Food-obsessed girls talk about food all the time, read cookbooks, and bake cakes for the family. They'll think, talk, and even dream about food—do everything but eat it. The struggle for control through dieting and the body distortions that arise create an ongoing cycle of weight loss and weight gain. So your daughter never gets to know what weight her body is comfortable with and she's never comfortable with her weight.

Q. What are the physical consequences of not eating right?

A. Weighing too much or too little can put a lot of stress on your daughter's body, even if you don't see it. Losing a lot of weight too fast can also put stress on her body. What

157

complicates this for you is that you're not actually seeing much of what your daughter eats or how she's dieting.

One of the easiest ways to talk to your daughter about eating right is to talk about the quality of her hair. Few girls are ever really happy with their hair, but girls who eat poorly have hair that's thin and dry and brittle. This is especially true for girls who have cut too much fat out of their diets. The other good indicator of a poor diet is the condition of their skin and nails. Pointing out that glossy hair, clear skin, and strong nails are best achieved through good nutrition and a healthful diet is an effective way to motivate your daughter to change.

Q. There's so much going on in her life. How can I tell if some problem is food-related?

A. It's natural to chalk up a lot of your daughter's behavior to typical adolescent mood swings, but you need to read between the lines. If she's really cranky and irritable and tells you it's because she had a fight with one of her best friends, it's possible that it's really that all she had to eat the whole day is a rice cake and a Diet Coke. There are real consequences to bad nutrition. The following signs can help you identify and head off possible trouble. (If you really have concerns, call a nutritionist or a specialist in adolescent medicine.)

Is she tired all the time? It could be iron deficiency, erratic eating, or just not eating enough. Or it could be not enough sleep, or even depression.

Is she low on energy? It could be a sheer lack of calories.

Is she so skinny that her ribs are showing? She doesn't weigh enough.

Does she always seem weak and tired? She could be skipping meals or not drinking enough water.

Does she have problems sleeping? She might be hungry. It could be that she's feeling too much pressure in her life. Or it could be depression.

Does she have problems concentrating? It could be lack of calories.

Is she really irritable? If she's cranky with her friends, not just you, you know it's a real problem. Again, she might need a more steady food intake.

Does she seem to catch every bug that's going around? Her lowered immunity could be the result of bad nutrition.

Is she sad and depressed? Crying a lot? Could be a boy, a test score, a bad diet. Could be anything.

Does she have frequent headaches? Often, this is from thirst.

DISORDERED EATING
ON THE VERGE OF OUT-OF-CONTROL

These red flags should alert you that your daughter needs your help:

Your daughter knows *everything* about nutrition.

Your daughter knows *nothing* about nutrition.

Your daughter can tell you the calorie count of every food on the dinner table. (An eating disorder is when she can tell you the calorie count of every food in the supermarket.)

It looks to you as if your daughter's diet for the day is way under 1,000 calories. Just when you're convinced she's anorexic, the next day it's over 4,000 calories.

You constantly hear your daughter say, "I'm not hungry" or "I just ate."

Your daughter weighs herself all the time. Or she doesn't want to know what she weighs because she can "absolutely tell" what she weighs just by looking in the mirror.

She lives on Frozfruit bars.

She says she's a vegetarian but she doesn't actually eat vegetables. (Well, pizza, pasta, Pepsi, and potato chips *are* vegetarian.)

She eats pizza without the crust, a bagel hollowed out, a salad without any dressing.

She and her friends know much too much about the fat grams in a cheese enchilada.

Chapter 9

<u>SEX</u>

BODY IMAGE IS, in essence, about sex. Being comfortable with your body and being sexually comfortable are strongly connected. As an adolescent girl struggles to gain a sense of comfort with her developing sexuality, she focuses even more intently on her body. One of her most important goals in adolescence is to integrate a positive body image with a sexual identity that works for her. To do that she needs to understand sex and her own sexuality—her sex appeal, what gives her pleasure, what attracts her to a sexual partner, how to put together a relationship that is fulfilling both emotionally and sexually.

Your goal, as a mother, is to help her figure all these issues out and put them in some perspective. Begin by trying to understand her world. However complicated sex was when you were growing up—whether it was needlessly secret and mysterious or filled with value judgments, whether you were overprotected or too free—it's much more complicated for your daughter. If you were exposed to too little, she is bombarded with sexually charged messages. If you had too many boundaries and inhibitions, she has been led to believe that anything goes. On top of that, the brief time an adolescent girl is given to figure out sex and sexuality puts her under tremendous pressure from society and from her friends. If you grew up thinking *no one* was having sex, she's growing up thinking that *everyone's* having sex, all the time. So she puts pressure on herself to grow up and catch up.

Girls today feel that there's a direct correlation between being popular and being sexually active. To be cool is to be sexual. Yet the double standard is still alive and well. Boys who are sexually active are considered to be experienced and mature. Girls who are sexually active are often considered to be whores and sluts. For boys, sex without commitment is considered fun, whereas for girls, it's considered promiscuity. And who perpetuates this way of thinking? Many people, including girls. Girls are often critical of each other, not to mention competitive. They're quick to deride the behavior of other girls whose sexual conduct may be exactly the same as their own. It's a way they can feel superior and an attempt to protect their own reputation.

So in our warp (and warped) speed world, where it seems easier to be liberated in the office than in the bedroom, girls aren't maturing emotionally any more quickly, but they are becoming sexually active much earlier. Wasn't it just last month that your daughter was styling Barbie's hair? What your daughter is doing at thirteen is what you may have done or been too scared to do at eighteen. Some mothers say, "To feel less crazy about what my daughter is doing, I just add five years to her age."

Between all the pressure, all the sensationalized sexual messages in the media, all the grapevine gossip and whispered misinformation, these girls, especially the youngest and most immature, don't know what to think or believe. They are much too embarrassed to talk to their mothers about sex. And yet, while a girl might be pushing her mother away harder than ever, she needs her mother's wisdom and experience more than ever. In truth, you have a vital role to play, and the more you understand what's happening to your daughter, the more effective you can be in mothering her.

First you have to understand what's going on with her body. A girl's physical development starts very early these days, usually between nine and a half and eleven. Early bloomers face all sorts of problems that relate to their sexuality. Girls who develop very early are vulnerable to having people think that they are ready for sexual invitations when they're nowhere near ready. They get attention they don't want. ("Hey, baby, wanna . . . ?") They don't know how to respond or even what they're responding to, so they feel vaguely creepy and guilty, as if their bodies were proof that they did something wrong. Girls who menstruate early are unprepared for the rapid physical changes (developing womanly breasts in a matter of months) and intensifying sexual sensations (an upsurge in masturbation). Confused and awkward, they can react in dramatic ways. Early changes can trigger feelings of disgust that make some girls want to retreat from social situations that involve boys or bathing suits; they become so self-conscious and modest that they cover up their bodies. Other girls react by becoming sexually provocative in ways even Lolita never explored.

In early adolescence many girls exhibit both types of behavior, so you never quite know who you're dealing with— Lolita or the shy, sweet thirteen-year-old who calls you Mom. Very immature girls who are still closely attached to their mothers often start acting out sexually. These girls can't find any other way to reconcile the conflict they feel between their almost childlike emotions and their maturing bodies.

Not surprisingly, more adventurous girls start acting out sexually, too. Girls who move more gradually into these new stages and who aren't the first ones in their group to go through them have an easier time adjusting. At this early stage of adolescence, most girls have an exaggerated idea of what it is to be sexual. Their need to display their sexuality and their bodies is a reflection of their insecurity. They develop body image problems because they expect to be fully developed and sexually active almost overnight.

With the rush of physical growth and all the hormonal changes, every girl has new sexual feelings, urges, sensations, fantasies. And this is not an either/or list: she'll have all of them, often all at once (lucky, lucky you). It's normal for her to start exploring her body through masturbation and to start having sexual encounters with boys. But what's age-appropriate and normal and healthy may not *feel* that way to her. Feeling comfortable in her body is suddenly an everyday challenge *and* a long-term process.

New ways of feeling and thinking about her body cause an

adolescent girl to start thinking about herself in new ways—as a person capable of having sex, of having a sexual relationship, of falling in love, of being desirable or not. She discovers new joys (kissing is fun, French kissing is *really* fun), new concerns (pregnancy and STDs), new fantasies ("A perfect body will make me sexy and then life will be perfect"), and new fears ("No one will want me if I'm fat").

It's clear that she needs help. She needs sex education, and not just from her girlfriends. She needs a shoulder to cry on. She needs to know that understanding sex and being sexual are processes that call for maturity and she's not yet mature. This is where you come in. While she needs good advice and information from lots of different sources, *you* are the best person to teach her about everything from romance to relationships to safe sex to what happens at frat parties after four zombies. Teaching doesn't mean you have to have every answer; it's okay to say, "Wow, that's a really tough question. Let me think about it." You don't have to know every technical detail: "Let's see, the vulva is important because, umm . . . it, uh . . ." You do need to be as open and honest about sex as you can be. Because there is so much anxiety in talking about sex, mothers (and daughters) tend to be indirect in their communication, talking about other people as examples ("Your friend Sasha is going to get some reputation"), making vague, offhand comments ("Be careful. Don't do anything I wouldn't do"), or only hinting at the real concern ("Isn't that top a little tight for school?").

Be candid and direct, not just with your daughter but with

yourself. Acknowledge your own fears and issues and hang-ups (everyone has some) and try to separate them from your daughter's concerns. You need to be able to tolerate some embarrassment. "Have I ever had a multiple orgasm? Well, that's another good question, honey . . ." If you can admit your ignorance ("She gave the football captain a BJ? That's nice. What's a BJ?"), acknowledge your embarrassment ("Oh, my God, I thought a BJ was a candy bar") and try to get with the program a little more, your daughter can see you as someone she can actually talk to. And she will talk to you more than you might expect, if you listen to her and then tell her what you think without being judgmental.

Let's face it. Every woman knows that having sex tends to be a lot easier than talking about it. You'll feel less awkward and shy, though, once you realize that communicating with your daughter about sex doesn't just mean talking to her. There are lots of nonverbal ways to get your ideas and information across, and you've probably been doing most of them without realizing it since your daughter was a baby. From the first time you picked her up and held her, you've given her a sense of the pleasures that the body holds. The way she's been loved and touched has given her a template for how she can love. Observing your physical connection with her father or your partner has given her a sense of the difference between touching, affection, and sexuality. Explaining to her the importance of privacy and the need for boundaries has helped her learn to respect her body. Of course, most important, you've communicated your values and standards.

Your spoken and unspoken messages have shaped your daughter's core ideas about sexuality and her sense of self. Have you always treated her like Little Miss Beauty Pageant Queen? Do you think it's a crime for any woman to go out of the house without makeup? Have you told your daughter how outraged you get when you see advertising that demeans women by showing them as sex objects? Do you think letting her watch an R-rated movie once in a while is no big deal? Are you okay with coed sleepovers? Do you think it's wrong for a girl to be too athletic? Think about it. Since she was a child, you and her father have given her a strong message about what you value in female sexuality and in relation to the opposite sex. Not surprisingly, by the time she is around nine or ten, it's pretty clear to your daughter whether you think that Pamela Anderson is a better example of evolved womanhood than Madeleine Albright.

Once your daughter hits puberty, it's time to take stock of what you've communicated, think about what she's taken in, see how it's affected her, and understand how it's a part of who she is. A good litmus test is to observe how *she* looks at sex and how she judges her body. Then ask yourself: Is she listening to what I say? Does she nod her head and then go off and do the opposite? Does she act as if sex isn't something she could think of discussing with you in her wildest dreams? Once you get a sense of where she is emotionally, you can gauge more accurately how to talk to her. To have any remote hope of being successful, you will need to decode what your daughter is saying. If you're smart and lucky, you'll learn not only what she's saying about sex but what she's thinking about herself and her body.

HOW TO DECODE WHAT SHE'S SAYING

ANNA: Mom, you don't understand how depressing it is to be with my friends who are so beautiful. They get all the attention from boys and I don't.

What she is really saying is that she feels pressure to be as attractive and sexual as her friends and she's enormously insecure about her looks. She needs you to be her compass, pointing her in the right direction and helping her to be less self-critical.

MARY ALICE: Boys think I'm just one of the guys. Maybe I'm a lesbian.

What she's really saying is that she's unsure of her sexuality or her sexual identity. You need to let her explore these questions about herself safely, which means listening to her calmly and not freaking out. Some girls are scared that they may be homosexual, so they jump into bed with the nearest guy to reassure themselves. Some start to identify with people who take a more liberal view of things and who are open about homosexuality and different sexual identities. Still other girls take on different sexual personas, having little understanding of what they mean. "I'm bisexual, transgendered, poly-sexed . . ." You name it, they try it on for size. You may want to suggest she speak with a counselor.

JILL: I *have* to pierce my belly button. Everyone at school is do-
       ing it. Do you want me to be the only one who's out of it?

What she's really talking about is defining herself by sending a message about her independence and sexuality. For many ado-lescent girls, piercing and tattooing are rites of passage—the hippest, coolest way of joining their generation. Use common sense. Talk with your daughter and figure out how important this step is to her and to you. Once you know why she wants to pierce her belly button, you can say yes or no. You can talk to her about other ways she can announce her coming of age. You might make a contract with her that when she reaches a certain age, if she still wants it, then she can do it. But don't think you can talk her out of it. About the best you can do is say some-thing like "This is what I would *like* you to do. But it's your body and you're in charge." Many girls will just go off and do it, precipitating a big falling-out with their mothers. If that's what your daughter does, think of it (when you have recovered sufficiently) as an opportunity to talk to her about your rela-tionship and her choices. Use it as a part of the process.

KAITLIN: He's so bad. He only goes out with hot girls. I wish
         he'd call me.

Welcome her to the wonderful world of women, where bad boys are much more appealing than suitably nice boys. Tell her not to totally abandon her common sense. Then tell her to have fun.

BRITTANY: Life sucks. I'll never look good in Victoria's Secret underwear.

This could mean lots of different things and maybe nothing at all. But look out for any signs of disordered eating, depression, or precocious sexuality. Your daughter doesn't think she measures up to hot, hot, hot lingerie models and she thinks she should.

ASHLEY: Mom, sex and love are just myths. Get over it. I don't even want a boyfriend.

She's saying that she's learning that sex and relationships don't have to go together. Listen a little more and you may hear that she's scared of disappointment and feels inadequate. She's afraid she won't be able to attract any boy she really likes. She wants you to think that times have changed and she's a free agent, but is she defensively turning her fear into a statement of liberation? Ask her to think of examples of strong, loving relationships.

FRAN: I can handle drinking. Having a few drinks is no big deal. I'm more relaxed. I have more fun, but I never get so drunk that I lose control or forget what I'm doing.

It's easy to overreact when it comes to drugs and drinking. It's actually hard *not* to. Every mother worries about addiction.

But it isn't just addiction you need to worry about. And worrying isn't going to help your daughter if she's got a real problem. If you really think there are signs that your daughter might have substance abuse problems, then you need to act. Get her help from a qualified teen drug counselor right away. If you feel that she's using drugs and alcohol to make herself more free socially and sexually, you need to be very clear about what can happen when her judgment is impaired. Help your daughter understand the social, medical, and legal consequences of everything from binge drinking to carrying false ID to drinking and driving. You also need to understand what the legal implications are for you.

ROSALIE: I only get attention from boys because they think
I'll put out. I'll never get a real boyfriend.

This is a girl with low self-esteem. A girl who feels this bad about herself feels pressure to get attention from boys by trading sexual favors. If this sounds like your daughter, you need to talk to her about valuing herself and her sexuality.

MELANIE: I'm hanging out with my friends at Emily's house.
A few guys are coming over. It's nothing big. Why do
you always want to know if her parents are at home?

Dating, as you think of it, is a thing of the past. She's letting you know how she and her friends get together with boys. Talk to her about the boundaries that you're comfortable with and try to balance those boundaries with what she thinks her busy social life requires. It's very important to keep this conversation going and not let it become a struggle for control.

After decoding what your daughter is saying to *you*, think about what you're saying to *her*, how you're saying it, and what (if anything) it means to her. In short, take responsibility for your part in this process. Many mothers are most comfortable talking restrictively about sex, highlighting fears, and dwelling on prohibitions. And while you obviously need to be clear about unprotected or dangerous sex, AIDS, and date rape, if you *only* talk judgmentally and restrictively about sex, your daughter will tune you out. If you scare her about sex, she'll react by making choices based on fear, not on what's best for her. A message that something is wrong with sex and with her will make her feel powerless. Your negative messages suggest that she doesn't have control over what happens with her body. Helping her understand herself and why she *is* in control will help her avoid feeling bad or overwhelmed. When she doesn't feel scared or overwhelmed, she's more likely to know when to say yes and when to say no.

When it comes to sex, your daughter doesn't have to say anything at all for you to understand a lot. By being observant, you can decode her look, her attitude, her reactions, her clothes, her protests. Girls express their thoughts, feelings, and problems about sex through their bodies. When a girl feels good about herself, you can see it in the care she takes in her appearance and in the pleasure she takes in her newfound sex appeal. Girls who are in trouble signal their problems in different ways. A girl may gain weight or diet strenuously. She may lose any sense of enjoyment of physical activities; this is the girl who stays home sick so she can watch the soaps and whose deepest boy relationship is with Chandler on *Friends*. Another girl will refuse to take her sexual behavior seriously and will ignore the consequences of anything she's doing. *Other* girls get pregnant or get sexually transmitted diseases, not her. Lastly, there is the girl who is happy to buy into every single sex myth she hears: "You can't get pregnant when you have your period." "You can't get AIDS from oral sex."

Conformity, including sexual conformity, is an important component of all adolescent behavior. Being thin and *looking* sexy are everything. Having—or *looking* like you have—experience is key. The fear of being sexually different is always there. The difficulty is that it's hard to conform when every adolescent girl develops at her own pace, in her own unique way. Girls don't have the experience or perspective to see this contradiction; they think everyone else is doing great and they're the only ones with a problem. Some girls handle this tension by expressing their insecurities to their friends. Others are too inhibited to talk about it.

If you think it's hard for your daughter to get some perspective and balance, it can be just as hard for you. Sex is the area where mothers are most likely to be "too" something. Some are too permissive. The mother most likely to let her daughter do just about anything is usually the one who is trying to compensate for her own sexually repressed adolescence. She gives her daughter "freedom." So why doesn't her daughter feel better about herself, her body, and her sexuality? Because she experiences this freedom as a lack of communication and mentoring. But when contemporary issues make you too confused to do or say anything, what you're really doing is failing to strike a balance between healthy parental limits and intrusiveness. When your daughter is anchored in solid values and knows what the rules are, life is easier for her. She can deal with situations better and take pressure off herself by using you as the heavy. She might say something to a boy like "I'd love to come over to your house, but my mother would kill me. I'd be grounded for a month, and I just couldn't handle that."

Some mothers are too anxious. They respond to the first signal that their daughter might be having sex by racing her off to the gynecologist for a checkup and birth control, whether or not their daughter asks for it. (By doing this, a mother is unwittingly giving her daughter the message that she *should* be sexually active.) These well-meaning mothers obviously want to protect her from an unwanted pregnancy; however, they may be assuming that she is already having intercourse when she's just beginning to explore sex.

Some mothers are too competitive. A mother may want her daughter to look good so that *she* looks good. Her daughter has to be thin and pretty and popular. She treats her daughter's boyfriend as if he's her own greatest accomplishment. She gossips with her friends about her daughter's relationships as if they were her own. While overly attentive to each and every detail of her daughter's popularity and romance, this mother tells her daughter almost nothing about sex. She assumes her daughter will learn that from her boyfriend and can't imagine that the girl would even want to discuss sex with her mother. After all, she herself never talked about it with *her* mother. Her daughter is likely to feel insecure and empty without a boyfriend; she's being set up to see her attractiveness as her ticket to success.

Some mothers are too protective. A mother may project her own problems with sex and relationships (such as divorce, abandonment, abuse) onto her daughter. She is scared that her daughter will be hurt by love, so she discourages her from looking sexual or becoming attached to any one boy. This mother is genuinely unaware of how directly her own issues influence her daughter's views and choices. The daughter is vulnerable to low self-esteem and body image issues, because her mother makes it hard for her to feel good about her sexual feelings and the attention she gets from boys.

Some mothers are too shy to talk about sex. A mother may have a hard time seeing her daughter grow up; she doesn't want to hear too much about what's going on. She figures her daughter will learn about sex in school or from her girlfriends, the same way she did, since she could never discuss sex with her own mother.

Finally, there are the mothers who are too eager to tell their daughters *everything*. This type sees her liberated attitude as the best assurance for averting "sexual hang-ups" in her daughter. She lets her daughter know that she *expects* her to be sexual. She unwittingly sends her daughter out into the world with the message "You're fourteen. You're a woman. Go for it."

When you talk to your daughter about sex:

- Let her know it's good to say no sometimes. She should always feel free to say no (with no reason and no apology) if something doesn't feel right.
- Let her know some of the positive things about sex (sex is pleasurable, fun, an expression of love) without sharing your sex life with her.
- Let her know that sex is more than a sexual act. It's the pleasure of desire, anticipation, affection, achieving intimacy, laughing when you're naked.
- Let her know that even outside of The Romance Channel movies and in spite of *Sex and the City*, sex still relates to love. All teenage girls are searching for love; romantic love is the most important affirmation of their sexuality and their sense of themselves as maturing young women.
- Let her know that she can experiment, explore, do things she might regret, and still feel empowered. It's her body and they're her choices. It's up to you to encourage her to take responsibility for these choices without lecturing her or being too overbearing. Whatever you have to say, it helps to start slowly and be as clear and straightforward as you can be. If you scare her because *you're* scared, or if you're in the habit of giving her dire warnings about everything in life, she will be much more likely to disregard your warnings about sex.

- Let her know that you're respecting her privacy. Add that if she gives you hints that things are troubling her, you'll be available and you'll follow up.
- Don't add to her problems. Be there for her. Let her know that if she's in trouble, she can come to you without your flipping out.
- Be a good role model. Enjoy your own sexuality. Be proud if you're lucky enough to be in a strong relationship or happy marriage.
- Let her know (if you're really comfortable with each other) that it's great to be frank and funny about sex.

And some things *not* to say:

- Don't provide more information than she's asking for.
- Don't give her reason to prove you're wrong. If you say, "You're much too young to go out with a senior. And you're way too naïve," you're practically inviting her to prove to you that she's a sexual person.
- Don't get too clinical or too crude about sex.
- Don't take a trip down memory lane unless you have a point relevant to her life.
- Don't be a stage mother about sex. Pushing her into something—whether it's a sexy pair of heels or a relationship with a boy—is courting disaster.
- Don't communicate your own hopes and dreams or your disappointments with men. She's her own person. You can't save her from all the regrettable things that happened to you.

- Don't turn every boyfriend into a son-in-law.
- Don't violate a confidence. Your daughter has to know she can trust you implicitly.

WHEN IT COMES TO SEX, your job is to answer your daughter's questions, respect her concerns, promote a healthy attitude, and know that her body image issues are the most reliable indication of how well she's dealing with her sexuality. Accept who she is sexually. Remember that a little common sense goes a long way. And try to relax enough to enjoy your daughter's sexuality. Admire her, laugh with her, feel great about how she looks.

TEN THINGS NEVER TO SAY
TO YOUR DAUGHTER ABOUT SEX

1. "Stop eating those Cheez Doodles or you'll never have a boyfriend." (Let her figure it out.)

2. "You did *what* with him?!" (You may *be* shocked, but *acting* shocked doesn't help.)

3. "Let's tell Daddy!" or, "What would Daddy say?" (Some things are between a mother and a daughter.)

4. "When *I* was your age . . ." (Who cares?)

5. "I hope you're using birth control. Would you like some condoms?" (Leave room for her to ask.)

6. "So what's Emily doing with Tom?" (Don't fish.)

7. "What boy will want to go out with you if you . . . ?" (This variation on "If you can get the milk for free, why buy the cow?" went out with the Dark Ages.)

8. "Honey, don't be so shy. Just call him up." (Pushy, pushy. Leave her alone.)

9. "*I* always had loads of boyfriends." (Don't be so competitive.)

10. "Don't worry about having a boyfriend. Take more tennis lessons. You'll have lots of time for boyfriends when you're in college." (Is this what *you* want or what *she* wants?)

Chapter 10

WHEN TO WORRY, WHEN TO INTERVENE, HOW TO HELP

SOME EMOTIONAL TURMOIL comes with the territory during adolescence, but there is a real difference between teenage angst and serious problems. It's difficult to know how to react to the current wave of issues daughters face: eating disorders, depression and suicide, cutting, drug use, school violence, dating violence. These issues may go far beyond anything that you had to deal with growing up. Some mothers react with so much anxiety that they either go into a state of denial and miss the cues of their daughters' problems completely, or go to the other extreme and turn into hypervigilant detectives seeing signs of trouble everywhere.

A mother in denial has a false sense of security that keeps her from seeing the signs and symptoms that signal trouble. When she discovers that her daughter's difficulty is serious, she is stunned. The situation usually has to get even worse for her to realize that help is needed.

The flip side of such denial is exemplified by the mother who turns detective and, looking for problems, always manages to find one. Her prying and worrying and her tendency to overreact are likely to drive her daughter away from her and damage their relationship. This girl sees her mother's concern as interference and resents it, so she will do just about anything to keep her out of the loop. And how can a girl trust a mother who seems not to trust her? The result is that when real problems arise, as they inevitably do, they can't be dealt with effectively.

Even mothers who are ready to listen, learn, and deal with their daughters' problems often have difficulty knowing how and when to intervene. Striking a balance between not-so-benign neglect and overvigilance isn't easy. Sometimes it isn't even easy to see *whose* problem you're dealing with. A family situation—anything from divorce to alcoholism to serious illness to moving to losing a job to family violence—will affect every member of your family, but none more acutely than your adolescent child. A problem doesn't have to involve her directly to have a huge impact on your daughter.

You may not even know she's suffering. Her response to what's going on may be a blithe "It's not *my* problem. What do I care?" But while she is the last one to acknowledge what she's feeling, she may be the first one to show it. Like the canary in the coal mine, your daughter may signal how serious a family problem is. And the way she is most likely to signal her pain is through her body.

These problems are expressed in different ways. A girl may feel pulled back into the family just when she's trying to separate. Reacting to a family that seems so disturbed and dysfunctional, she may feel that *someone* needs to look like they have it together, so she becomes obsessed with her body's attractiveness—the one area she thinks she can control. Another girl may be so thrown by family problems that she acts out her despair by giving up on her looks. She risks becoming obese or turning to drugs or having unprotected sex. The irony in these situations is that because their behavior sets off the alarm bells, these girls, who are *reacting* to their family's problems, often get blamed for having *caused* them. Labeling these girls as the ones who need help, when in fact the whole family needs help, makes them justifiably angry and resistant to getting any help at all.

Be smart: separate your family's issues from your daughter's issues. Try to create an atmosphere at home in which all kinds of problems can be discussed without fear of shame or reprisal. Remember that being alert isn't the same as worrying. Assigning blame doesn't help either. Once you know there's a problem, the right question to ask is "How can we solve this?" But when the signs aren't as clear as, say, a huge weight gain or bottles missing from your liquor cabinet, how do you know your daughter is in distress and isn't coping?

First, educate yourself to recognize the warning signs. Learn the classic textbook signs of emotional problems. Then look for whatever your daughter's own personal red flags are. If, for example, she's always been a good eater and now she's never hungry, that's a red flag. Learn what steps to take if she needs help and where to get it.

Then be prepared for resistance. Some girls may ask for help easily, but it is more common for a girl to hide her problems out of fear that she will be ridiculed, blamed, stigmatized, or treated like a child. She may refuse help because she is overwhelmed with guilt and shame. Or, as girls often do, she may defensively deny her problem, then project blame onto you or someone else and refuse to admit that an issue even exists. This type of fierce resistance is very hard to break through.

Doing everything you can to help your daughter get professional help from a psychotherapist, nutritionist, doctor, or teen health center is as essential to your role as a mother as making sure she goes to school regularly and gets enough sleep. "Doing everything" for her doesn't include:

- Bribery, which never works.
- Manipulation, which is just as ineffective.
- Trying to trick her by telling her you're going to therapy for someone else in the family.

Be honest with your daughter. Be willing to face even the most painful issues and make it possible for all of you to acknowledge the part you play in the problem. It's essential to create enough trust to allow her to work on the problem with you.

Here are some of the most commonly experienced emotional problems that affect teenage girls. Some start in childhood; others have genetic components that become more

complicated because of the physical, hormonal, and psychological changes an adolescent girl goes through. Most come
from her adjusting to adolescence and striving for maturity.

ANXIETY DISORDERS

How do you recognize an anxiety disorder? An *anxiety disorder*
is fear that explodes, becomes irrational, and starts to have a
life of its own. Normal fear (or anxiety) is the reaction that
prompts us to get out of the way of a speeding car. An anxiety
disorder is getting out of the way of a speeding car, then thinking that every car you see in the future is going to hit you.

Anxiety disorders include generalized anxiety, phobias,
obsessive-compulsive disorders, panic attacks, and stress disorders. The common thread is excessive fear, which causes
the kind of persistent worry that dominates both thoughts
and behavior. In an anxiety disorder, unrealistic fears are
unable to be assuaged by common sense and reasoning.

Teenagers frequently exhibit normal fear as a consequence
of situations that are new to them. Their inexperience and
immaturity don't equip them to deal with, say, going to a
party where they don't know anyone or being called on to
read a personal essay to a class of forty strangers. This type of
anxiety should not be a source of concern.

You *do* need to be concerned if your daughter seems overwhelmed and is coping with her anxiety in self-destructive
and self-defeating ways. If this pattern of behavior becomes
clear to you (and hopefully to her), it's time to get help. An

appropriate intervention at this time will go a long way toward reducing her suffering and averting long-term emotional problems.

Types of Anxiety Disorders

Generalized Anxiety Disorder is the term applied to feelings of worry and fear that are present for several months and that are not specific to any one particular stressful situation. Generalized anxiety produces the following five symptoms and warning signs. A girl suffering from generalized anxiety may have one or more of these:

1. She's restless and fidgety. She feels on edge, irritable, and tense. For example, she's nervously focused on her body and blames all of her problems on her body, but if anyone makes a suggestion that might help her feel better, she blows up, angrily accusing them of saying she's ugly.

2. She has difficulty concentrating and in some cases her mind goes blank. She may experience test anxiety, forget basic information, confuse times and dates, or space out on her responsibilities. She's not able to make decisions and she becomes immobilized, anticipating that something will go wrong.

3. She has problems sleeping. She complains of insomnia, bad dreams, and waking in the middle of the night. Her sleep patterns are disturbed and she is likely to sleep all day and be awake all night.

4. She is extremely shy and ill at ease around people. This is a girl who wants to "disappear" and who blames her shyness on something that has to do with her looks, such as not having the right clothes or not being as thin as other girls.

5. She avoids new situations, even if they seem as though they might give her pleasure. She makes excuses about why she can't go out: her hair doesn't look right or she doesn't fit into her good jeans. She's so self-conscious that she imagines people are looking at her judgmentally, which makes her feel even more unattractive.

A *phobia* is a type of anxiety disorder in which persistent, intense fears occur in response to a specific stimulus and an unconscious forbidden wish. Sometimes a phobia will emerge in response to a traumatic situation (divorce, death of a parent, loss of a best friend). Many teenagers develop mild phobias in response to stress. These disappear as the teenagers gain life experience and coping skills.

More serious phobic reactions actually restrict functioning and can become crippling. These are *panic attacks, acute stress disorders*, and *post-traumatic stress disorders (PTSD)*. When a girl suffers from panic attacks and stress disorders, she experiences acute emotional anxiety along with physical symptoms so severe that they make her feel that she is sick, having a heart attack, or about to die. Panic attacks occur suddenly, seemingly out of the blue, without any specific trigger, and may involve flashbacks of the traumatic event. They can occur once or multiple times.

In trying to cope with panic attacks and stress disorders, girls may try to control their feelings and thoughts by developing behaviors aimed at warding off memories and feelings associated with the trauma they suffered. This is often the origin of eating disorders, cutting, and other body image disturbances. What's vitally important to understand is that these self-destructive behaviors represent for these girls a *solution*, a way to control events, thoughts, and feelings that would otherwise overwhelm them. Eating disorders in particular have been linked to sexual abuse and incest.

A girl who has uncontrollable anxious thoughts can, in an attempt to control or get rid of nagging fears, develop behavior that is termed *obsessive-compulsive*. This girl feels compelled to do or say ritualized things aimed at controlling these thoughts and fears. She's afraid that if she fails to perform some ritual (praying, counting, repeating words silently, checking and rechecking things such as a light that should be left on), something bad will happen to her or someone she loves. These behaviors can take over her life. Depression frequently accompanies this problem because fending off torturous fears is exhausting and unending. As "magic" rituals, obsessive-compulsive thoughts and behaviors are particularly common in girls with body image problems. They are an important component of eating disorders and disordered eating.

A common obsessive-compulsive disorder that relates to

severe body image disturbance is called *body dismorphic disorder*. This syndrome occurs when a girl imagines that some feature of her face or some part of her body is extremely ugly. Convinced that something is severely wrong, she becomes obsessed by these imagined imperfections. An example of this is a girl who decides her neck is ugly and that she has to wear scarves or turtleneck sweaters to cover it up, no matter how inappropriate this might be. Eventually she becomes unable to socialize at school, limits her activities, and withdraws. No amount of reassurance will reduce the problem for her. Even successful plastic surgery won't overcome the underlying emotional problems. If these are not treated, she'll transfer her obsessions to some other part of the body. This type of emotional problem requires psychiatric treatment.

If you think your daughter has any kind of anxiety disorder:

1. Talk with your daughter before you talk with anyone else, if she will let you. Let her know that you see her behaving in self-destructive or self-defeating ways. *Be specific.*

2. Ask her questions based on what you have observed.

MOTHER: I heard you crying; what's troubling you? You seem so worried all the time.

BECKY: Nothing.

MOTHER: You may not want to tell me, but crying is a sign of something. And you may not want to talk about it now, but I'm here when you're ready.

3. Ask your daughter to be honest and evaluate the problem herself. If she denies that there is one, tell her that you disagree and that you'll bring it up again later. Don't continue to talk about it, point out the symptoms, or nag her about it. On the other hand, don't sweep it under the rug.

4. Present her with ways you could help and ask her opinion about these options. Give her choices, but don't give her a "Do nothing" choice.

5. If she tells you that the issue is something outside of her control—a situation at school, a blowup with her best friend, a boy who's dumped her—and that she's doing the best she can, let her know that she doesn't have to face things alone. She can get help.

6. Encourage her to see ways she can take control. Discourage her from blaming others, as in, "I would be fine if you and Daddy would stop putting pressure on me."

7. Take action. Don't put it off. Use your network. Talk with friends you trust, with doctors, clergy, school counselors. Find the good resources in your community and connect your daughter with the treatment she needs.

DEPRESSION

Your adolescent daughter is likely to think that depression is a bad mood caused by some immediate problem that's beyond her control. "I'm *sooo* depressed," for her, covers everything from hating the way she looks to breaking up with her boyfriend to her PMS to the death of her grandmother. You need to know the difference between a transient bad mood and true depression.

Depression is a complex disorder that has different variations. It is experienced both physically and mentally and is marked by biochemical changes in the brain that cause profound changes in mood and behavior. Depression results from feelings of hopelessness, helplessness, despair, and anger that is turned inward. ("I hate myself, I'm such a loser. There's no hope; I'm so ugly, I might as well just give up.") Teenage girls tend to attach these negative feelings to their body image and sexuality. There are strong genetic and environmental influences that increase the chance of suffering from depression. Girls who are genetically prone to depression don't have to have any outside stimulus to experience it. There is usually a family history of depression. Here are the main forms:

Mild depression (dysthymia) goes on for an extended period of time and can be treated with psychotherapy and antidepressant medication.

❧

Major depression can occur in a single episode or become chronic. It is a physical and psychological disease. There's a wide range of symptoms, from mild to extremely serious: everything from sleep disturbances to increased social isolation to loss of pleasure in familiar things to suicidal thoughts and actions.

191

Manic depression (bipolar disorder) involves depression and mania. The lows are very low and the highs range from an elevated mood to euphoria to grandiose thinking and racing thoughts. It must be treated with medication and therapy.

Complicated bereavement is just what it sounds like, a depression that follows the loss of a significant person— the death of a parent, a divorce, a friend's moving away, moving, the illness of a parent or sibling.

Dual diagnosis is the combination of depression with drug or alcohol abuse or addiction.

It's not always easy to spot a depressed teenager; doctors often misdiagnose depression in adolescents. Adults who are depressed *look* depressed; teens don't always. On the surface a girl may look remarkably cheerful and optimistic—almost too much so. Her sadness and emotional pain are hidden from everyone's view, including her own. Her depression comes out in edgy attitudes and dangerous behavior, such as delinquency (shoplifting or credit card theft), promiscuity, and drug and alcohol use. Because she is trying not to feel the emotional pain of depression, she puts all of her energy into action, which serves as an emotional diversion. At the same time, it sends the wrong signal to others. A depressed girl often feels that "no one gets it" and "no one cares," thinking,

"They just want me to be happy all the time." Angry that she is so misunderstood, she hides her real feelings and distrusts even people who care very much about her.

How deceptive can depression be? Take the girl who really doesn't *feel* depressed: if you ask her, she'll tell you she just feels that she's too fat. Her solution is to diet and exercise constantly in the hope of losing thirty or forty pounds. When she's not able to carry out this unrealistic plan, she loses hope and impulsively tries to kill herself. Does she feel depressed? No, she just hates the way she looks and doesn't want to live unless she's thin. She's completely disconnected from her feelings and is instead connected to a radically distorted body image.

It's important to remember with a vulnerable adolescent that without anyone's awareness all of the elements of depression are present and may appear quite suddenly. This is evident in the all-too-frequent expressions of shock that follow a teen suicide: "She was always such a happy kid," or, "How could that happen? She had so much going for her."

Red Flags for Depression

Some of the most common signs of depression in an adolescent girl are:

A depressed mood, sudden loss of interest in her appearance, lack of self-care, loss of sexual interest, fatigue, lack of energy, sleep disturbances, restlessness, appetite disturbance (eating too much or too little), crying for no reason, diminished interest in things that used to give her pleasure.

❧

Low self-esteem, lots of self-criticism, feelings of guilt; she takes responsibility for everything. Or she is the perpetual scapegoat or victim.

❧

Self-mutilation; cutting or burning herself intentionally.

❧

Hypochondria and psychosomatic illness. Frequent physical illness or a tendency to be accident-prone that makes it impossible for her to participate in regular activities.

❧

Acting-out behavior. This could be anything from cutting school to being uncharacteristically aggressive to promiscuity to shoplifting.

❧

Social withdrawal and isolation.

❧

Low frustration threshold, low tolerance, poor motivation, underachievement in school.

❧

Pessimism or hopelessness about the future.

❧

Preoccupation with thoughts of death or suicide. She says things like "Life is not worth living" or "Everyone would be better off without me around."

SUICIDE

Suicide is closely linked to depression. A suicidal girl wishes to die because she perceives death to be the only solution to her unendurable problems. Her hopelessness can come in response to an immediate loss, such as the breakup of a relationship ("I can't live without him"). It can be triggered by anything from the death of a beloved grandmother to the loss of an important goal (an "important goal" can be getting into the right college or going to the prom). Gender identity disorders or feelings of homosexuality may seem so threatening and so unacceptable that they lead to suicidal impulses. Ending psychotherapy or a recent recovery from addiction can, too: these are especially vulnerable times for a girl who is depressed because she is extremely fragile and uncertain that she really can feel better and stay healthy.

Red Flags for Suicide

Whatever the trigger, an adolescent girl's extreme feelings of helplessness and her enormous anger make her want to demonstrate her pain to the world by a suicidal gesture. She actually gets a sense of satisfaction from the attempt, imagining that she will punish others by her death. This grandiose idea to hurt herself can often occur without her ever imagining that she will actually die as a result.

You should know that girls attempt suicide four times more often than boys and are more likely to make impulsive suicidal gestures. Girls are more likely to leave hints, write letters or e-mails, announce their intentions, or say something to a friend, so you must pay attention to any signs whatsoever, even the smallest. Since many of these girls tend to be more dramatic and emotional than most, you may think that it's just talk, another way for them to add some drama to life. That's not the case with suicide. A girl's talking about it or even romanticizing it (loving movies like *The Virgin Suicides* or totally identifying with Sylvia Plath's poems) doesn't mean she won't do it; on the contrary, there is a high correlation between talking about wanting to die and making a suicide attempt. A girl who tries to commit suicide once probably will try it again.

CUTTING

Cutting is also closely linked to depression. Cutting doesn't mean body piercing or tattooing. It is self-mutilation: a girl will take a razor or something else sharp and nick or make incisions somewhere on her body, such as her arm or wrist. Cutting injuries aren't meant to be fatal. The girl who cuts is often not aware of feeling depressed. These girls often report that they can't *feel* their feelings and so they cut themselves in order to feel *something*. The reality is that they have many feelings but can't express them any other way. When those feelings are bottled up and ready to explode, cutting is her way to release them. Girls report a sense of tension immediately before they cut and a strong sense of relaxation and gratification immediately afterwards. These girls become numb to their physical pain.

Many girls engage in this behavior only at times of stress, and they protest that they will never do it again. If this is your daughter, *don't* believe that this is the last time she will do this to herself. Like suicide attempts, cutting is rarely an isolated incident. A girl may have good intentions, but the need to continue self-mutilation is difficult to extinguish without professional help and medication.

Red Flags for Cutting

Her skin shows signs of recurrent cutting or burning.

She tries to hide her cuts. A sense of shame and the fear of stigma lead her to wear long sleeves and big sweatshirts even in warm weather, to lie about the reason for her scars, and generally to behave with secrecy to cover up the evidence.

She's visiting the Web sites of "cutters," and she can repeat characteristics of the syndrome from memory.

EATING DISORDERS AND OBESITY

Disordered eating can range from constant dieting or binge eating to a life of fad diets or obsessing over calories and fat grams. *Eating disorders* are defined as the misuse of food to resolve emotional problems. An eating disorder is much more about the emotion than it is about the food.

Anorexia and bulimia are the two most common eating disorders. *Anorexia* is the constant restriction and denial of food to prevent weight gain. This restriction causes self-starvation. *Bulimia* is the intentional throwing up of food after it is eaten to avoid weight gain. Anorexia and bulimia are combined as a disorder when a girl is unable to maintain the extremely restrictive diet she has put herself on, eats food, then throws up immediately afterwards.

Eating disorders have become so common that many girls see them as an adolescent rite of passage. Unwittingly, they fall into a trap that proves very hard to climb out of. Girls who have eating disorders are typically able to keep them well hidden from the eyes of parents, teachers, and friends. They are, in the words of an eighteen-year-old girl who knows from experience, "excellent liars and great at keeping secrets."

Eating disorders can be one of the most destructive emotional problems to affect adolescent girls, because they can result in death or permanent physical harm. Severe eating disorders are likely to get such a grip on a girl's psyche that they can be as difficult to deal with as drug addiction. However, with early detection, the rate of cure is 80 percent.

Eating disorders have many causes; there is never one single reason, nor is there one simple cure. There is no one profile of a girl who suffers from an eating disorder. Typically, though, girls with eating disorders are highly intelligent, obedient, excellent students who are perfectionist, compulsive, and driven to excel.

Eating disorders may start in early adolescence, with a bright, sensitive girl who has fears about growing up and maturing sexually. She may have a problem with being over-weight and feel betrayed by her body. She may have gotten strong messages from her mother about how important it is to be thin. She may come from a family where eating disorders are already present. She may have a fragile sense of herself and be easily influenced by fashion magazines, TV, and movies. She figures out that if she stops eating, she will get what she wants: control over her body and approval for being perfect in a new way.

The girl diets consciously to lose weight, and unconsciously to rid herself of the breasts, hips, and round shape that are associated with becoming mature. When she restricts food intake, drops her body weight, loses body fat, and stops her period, she feels successful. She has found the enemy and it is *fat*. What is health-threatening behavior turns, in her mind, into an ingenious solution. Her terror of being fat becomes her means for dealing with all the conflicts she has—whether it's her fear of being a woman, the difficulty she's having separating from her mother, a troubled relationship with her father, or a way of numbing herself to family issues too difficult for her to deal with. She doesn't think she has a problem. She thinks she has a mission.

There is a common factor in girls who develop eating disorders: in childhood they were much loved and admired, but with adolescence everything changed. The deep unhappiness they feel inside becomes focused on their body image: they are too short or too tall, their hair is too curly or too straight. To gain control over these feelings they don't know how to express, they try to control their body by restricting food intake, eating no fat, throwing up after eating, bingeing then purging, all with the idea "If only I were thin, I'd be happy." They begin to diet successfully (these girls are successful at *everything*) and lose weight. They get positive attention and praise. And, in essence, they swallow their feelings.

As they get better at restricting their intake of food, their health gets worse. In time they lose perspective and have no sense of their bodies, of how little they weigh, of what they look like. They are even more disconnected from their feelings than they were before. Eventually their body image becomes so distorted that no matter how thin they are, they look fat to their own eyes.

Obesity

Many of the underlying emotional problems that lead to anorexia and bulimia are the same in girls who develop obesity. A girl is considered obese when she has 30 percent of excessive body fat in relation to the rest of her body. Medically, this is called the body mass index (BMI), and it can be measured by your doctor.

In a culture of thinness, adolescent girls who are overweight are subjected to endless criticism and ridicule. They hear well-meaning but insensitive comments, such as "You would be so much happier if only you would lose weight," or just plain insensitive ones, like "You say you're on a diet, but you're getting fatter. You *must* be cheating." They are told in words and with looks of disdain that they are undesirable and unwanted, so the self-loathing that develops in them is inevitable.

Many times these overweight girls will say they like the way they look, but few actually do. Most lose weight and then quickly regain it because the underlying emotional causes of their overeating are not addressed and because it is so difficult to change eating patterns permanently.

Red Flags for Eating Disorders

Sustained and profound unhappiness with physical appearance.

❧

Depression, irritability, isolation from others.

❧

Fear of eating in front of others. Refusing to eat what others are eating, not wanting to eat with you, never enjoying what she's eating.

❧

Restricting the amounts or types of foods that she eats. A kind of militant irrationality about food.

❧

Being hypersensitive to any comment you make about her eating. She will snap your head off for suggesting something innocuous about her health or her eating habits.

❧

Demonstrating food quirks, like drinking lots of water before meals, cutting food into tiny pieces, chewing slowly.

❧

Being really rigid about the times she'll eat or the order in which food is consumed.

❧

Saying she has a stomachache or a headache, or making some other excuse before family meals.

❧

Lying about how much she's eaten or what she's had all day or how much she weighs.

❧

Telling you what she thinks you want to hear and making endless excuses: she's just too tired to eat, she's under too much stress at school, the food at school is awful, etc.

Girls Who Are at Risk for Eating Disorders

While every girl's problem is different, there are some common risk factors. At least one of the following factors is present in every case:

- A girl is a perfectionist, highly self-critical, very competitive.
- There is addictive behavior (alcoholism, drugs) in the girl or in the family.
- The family has a history of depression.
- A mother or sister has an eating disorder or disordered thinking about her looks.
- A girl has low self-esteem (both the cause and the result of her eating disorder).

- A girl can't express her emotions or share her feelings.
- A girl has suffered some early sexual trauma (abuse, rape, assault).
- A girl's family dynamic is drastically troubled: no boundaries, no stability, great conflict, one parent far too strong and one far too weak. Behind every girl with an eating disorder, there is *always* some unresolved family issue.

Steps You Can Take with All Eating Disorder Problems

Be observant and alert. Confront your daughter with your observations. Give her a chance to talk about her feelings. Expect denial and secrecy. Be patient.

❧

Understand that she is hiding her behavior and her unhappy feelings from herself as well as from you. Since her eating disorder is her solution, she will resist your interference and the threat that you will take it away.

❧

Get educated about eating disorders and educate your daughter. Find professional help from a psychotherapist, a doctor, a qualified nutritionist, or a center for eating disorders. If she won't go at first, then *you* go. Start the process. You need guidance and support as well.

❧

Be open to anything and everything: individual therapy, family therapy, medication. Consider all of your options.

❧

Respect her privacy, but don't keep the situation a secret from the people you love and trust. Depression, anxiety, eating disorders, sexual identity issues, and behavior problems can all be treated. Don't stigmatize her for having a problem.

❧

Confidentiality is very important to the success of your daughter's therapy. Discuss the boundaries of confidentiality with her medical doctor or therapist and consider ways in which you and the family can be involved in her treatment.

❧

Be willing to take responsibility for anything you might have done to contribute to her problem. Remember that it isn't just *her* problem.

❧

Knowing that you and your daughter are not alone and that your family can admit that you *all* need help is the first step on the road to recovery.

DATING VIOLENCE

The truth is that dating violence occurs in as many as *one-third* of all teen relationships. *Dating violence* means anything from physical abuse to emotional abuse, and it crosses all economic and social boundaries.

Red Flags for Dating Violence

She has a relationship with a boyfriend (or girlfriend) that is characterized by dominance, possessiveness, and control. If you say anything critical, she defends him/her.

❧

She starts to diet or gain weight because her boy(girl)-friend wants her to. She changes the way she dresses for the same reason.

❧

You see radical changes in her behavior or study habits.

❧

She's isolated from her friends.

❧

Her boy(girl)friend seems "too good to be true." You may mistakenly feel that your daughter's boyfriend, for instance, is a good influence because he has greater control over her than you do. Without your knowing it, he maintains this control through constant criticism, belittling remarks, threats to leave, physical threats, or violent abuse.

TEEN PREGNANCY

The rate of teen pregnancy is probably higher than you think: 20 percent of sexually active girls aged fifteen to nineteen get pregnant each year, according to the Kaiser Family Foundation. In most cases these pregnancies are mistakes or the result of accidents. But sometimes they are intentional. Intentional pregnancies occur most commonly when girls are suffering from depression, family problems, and poor self-esteem. Anxiety and other types of personality disorders are also part of the picture. As with suicide and eating disorders, many girls see having a baby as a solution. They want someone to love them, and they imagine that a baby can fill up the emotional void in their life. A girl who has a poor body image and low self-esteem may believe that pregnancy will be a way to hold on to a boy or get him to marry her.

These girls are very vulnerable, resistant to help, and too afraid to admit that they are frightened. Both the mothers of these girls and the girls themselves need sensitive counseling from qualified professionals.

OTHER PROBLEMS OF SEXUAL HEALTH

It's a given that all teenage girls today are at risk as they enter into sexual relationships. It may be difficult for you to discern when problems are serious, because adolescent girls and their parents have a vastly different context when it comes to thinking and talking about sex and sexuality. Girls, for example, see their sexual experimentation and exploration as a positive growth experience. Parents, on the other hand, are more likely to focus on the risks involved and the potential consequences.

For parents and teens, even what sex *is* is up for debate. "Hooking up" (getting sexually connected in a disconnected way) is what a teenage girl today is likely to see as normal, while her mother perceives it as just plain casual, promiscuous sex. The most popular way of hooking up is oral sex, which, to one-half of all teens in America today, has come to mean "safe" sex. To their way of thinking, it's safer because it's not even "real" sex. "Real" sex—intercourse—is what's dangerous. The problem is that their "safe" sex practices—besides oral sex, there's anal sex and group sex—are wildly *un*safe. Girls who participate are at risk for physical problems (STDs like gonorrhea of the throat and genital herpes), for psychological problems (such as sexual identity confusion and eating disorders), and for social problems (such as being labeled "promiscuous" or feeling like a loser for not "putting out").

Pornography, in your daughter's world, is something parents get hysterical about and try to keep their kids from seeing on the Internet. Internet chat rooms are, to her way of thinking, the best way to connect with her friends and make new ones. And while in some ways chat rooms are no more risky than a blind date, it's clear that there *are* sexual predators (both adult and teenage) online who present a real (and growing) risk, especially for a vulnerable girl. Most parental controls are easily subverted by a determined girl. Most girls (surprise!) are determined. The posting of pictures, personal information, and explicit sexual come-ons can entice passive, insecure girls who want both romance and adventure. Girls who are more aggressive but equally insecure have no problem posting their own pictures and journals online and initiating these encounters themselves.

The bottom line is that both types of girls are willing to

take huge risks to increase their popularity and become sure of their sexuality. Confused and often feeling cut off from real-world sexual expression, they imagine themselves to be unattractive, fat, undesirable. The cachet and excitement of their edgy cyber encounters feels, to them, as if they've made a conquest and found a safe solution to their problems, all at once.

When it comes to gender issues and sexual identity, many girls today look at bisexuality and homosexuality as exciting ways to experiment and explore. But as with every other kind of experimentation, what they see as options, their parents are more likely to see as potential problems.

For lesbian girls who are just beginning to understand their sexuality, this can also be a time of turmoil. A healthy sexual adjustment depends on a girl's ability to access good sex education and adult guidance. When a girl who has questions about her sexual orientation is able to find understanding in her family and community, she will make a better adjustment. Even in communities enlightened enough to have gay and lesbian school organizations, parents need to be mindful of gay prejudice and become strong advocates for their daughter.

Girls Who Are at Risk in Their Sexuality

All girls are at risk, but some are more vulnerable than others. Who are they and why?

While family history, parental attitudes, and parents' comfort with their own sexuality are good predictors of how their

daughter will adjust to her sexuality, there are also some specific risk factors:

A girl is at risk when there's a family history of sexual
abuse or when she's witnessed inappropriate displays of
sexuality at home (such as pornography in the house).

❧

Girls who have lost their mothers through death, abandonment, illness, or divorce may be unable to identify
with a consistent mother figure. These girls can be desperate to establish relationships with boys or men to
replace the maternal attention and affection they've lost.

❧

As opposed to the girls who are just experimenting with
gender issues, a girl who feels she really might be homosexual can be at risk. As she struggles with her sexual
identity, she can panic and overreact, throwing herself
into a frenzy of high-risk sexual activity, both homosexual and heterosexual.

❧

Girls whose parents are homophobic and who express
their dismay at the possibility of their daughter's being
homosexual interfere with her ability to develop a clear,
positive sexual self. Their condemnation only adds to
her own sexual confusion and pain.

❧

Girls with overprotective and insecure parents who try
to control their daughters' sexual behavior by instilling

fear ("If you get in trouble with that boy, don't come to me") and issuing reprisals ("If you have sex too early and get a reputation, you'll never have a decent boyfriend") feel alone, unfairly judged, and unable to go to their parents with questions and problems.

And what exactly are girls most at risk *for?* What will their most extreme behavior lead to? What are the physical, social, and psychological risks?

- Unprotected sex can lead to unwanted pregnancy and STDs (sexually transmitted diseases), including viral infections such as HIV, AIDS, herpes simplex, hepatitis B, and genital warts; bacterial infections such as chlamydia, syphilis, vaginitis, and gonorrhea; fungal infections such as candida; parasites such as pubic lice (crabs) and scabies; and PID (pelvic inflammatory disease).
- High-risk sexual behavior can leave a girl vulnerable to rape, acquaintance rape, or sexual encounters that involve violence or physical harm. It can also increase her vulnerability to sexual predators.
- Sexual confusion can lead to sexual obsession, which at its most extreme can result in her stalking or being stalked— whether in person or on the Internet.
- Abuse of drugs and alcohol can reduce her inhibitions and lead to lack of judgment as well as loss of control. If a girl can blame her behavior on substance abuse, then it's not her responsibility and the consequences are not her fault.

She sets up a pattern of victimization for herself for the future.

- Premature sexual activity (between the ages of ten and thirteen) leads to increases in all risk factors. Precocious girls this age can be very aggressive sexually.

- Unhealthy sexual practices have long-term psychological consequences for adolescents. When they get older, these girls often have difficulty establishing a positive sex life.

Red Flags for Sexual Health Problems

Teenage girls are adept at keeping mothers at a distance until things reel out of control. Then you get to pick up the pieces. Your daughter may give you so many mixed signals that you don't know what's really going on, what's serious, or when there's a real problem. But there are some warning signs to look for:

She is secretive about her sexual activities. You can't get a straight answer about anything. She's often manipulative, and you are constantly catching her in lies. It's likely that she has something to hide from you as well as from herself. If she acts extremely defensive toward you, it's likely that she fears your judgment about some aspect of her sexual conduct.

❧

Your "good" girl starts acting like a "bad" girl, cutting class, maybe even shoplifting. Essentially, she exhibits poor judgment all around. The possibility is that she's acting out because she's feeling guilty and out of control about sex.

❧

She's showing more aggressive, self-hating behavior focused on her body. Again, this behavior suggests some problem and insecurity having to do with boys and sex.

❧

She's unable to recover from breaking up with a boyfriend, which may indicate that she is too immature to handle a sexual relationship.

❧

She accepts disrespectful treatment from boyfriends. This is another behavior that can easily set up a potential long-term problem.

This is a risky time for your daughter, and the more available you are to her, the greater the likelihood that she will seek you out when she is troubled and needs help. The most important thing you can do is to educate yourself about sexual health issues, know what's going on in her world, and pay attention to her. Reaffirm your own values to her and listen to her ideas. If you are unable to talk to her, too anxious, or too intrusive, you will only succeed in driving yourself crazy and driving her away. Once you drive her away, you may find out about a problem only when a crisis occurs.

There's another reason your involvement is crucial. Adolescent girls may be obsessed with their bodies, but paradoxically, they ignore symptoms that should tell them that something is wrong. In some cases they don't have the knowledge of their bodies or the experience to recognize that there is something wrong. Their embarrassment, along with their fear of your judgment, contributes to their minimizing their problems, denying them, and just hoping they'll go away. Your daughter may be in denial, but don't keep yourself from knowing.

Probably the easiest way for you to get a quick sex education course is to read a book such as *Healthy Teens, Body and Soul,* by Andrea Marks, M.D., and Betty Rothbart, M.S.W., or go to an Internet site such as Columbia University's www.goaskalice. columbia.edu or Rutgers University's www.sxetc.org, where you can get current information and read some candid personal journals.

HOW TO HELP WITH ACUTE PROBLEMS

It's important to know that as a rule of thumb, teenage girls who are in dire straits are likely to be the ones most ferocious in their resistance to go for help. If this is the case, her parents need to take charge and do whatever it takes to get her the help she needs. As a parent, you are obviously legally responsible for your daughter. But more important, as a *caring* parent, you must sometimes make very difficult decisions to help her.

Acute problems require immediate intervention: use your local hospital emergency room, telephone hot line, or mobile crisis team. Teen outreach programs can assist with girls who have run away from home. Psychiatric hospitals and drug treatment programs should be chosen on the basis of whether they have a unit that specializes in treating adolescents.

It's impossible for you to know what's going on in your daughter's head. All you can do is stay involved with her, observe her, and remember who she is even when she appears so different to herself and everyone else. Anticipate how hard it is for her to admit that she has a problem, let alone how hard it is to let you see even some of it. Remember that her resistance isn't just stubbornness, it's a defense against her fear that if she has to confront this huge problem, she will be completely overwhelmed by it.

This is a delicate and painful time. Sometimes it seems impossible to say or do the right thing. Be patient, and keep listening. Don't be afraid to confront your daughter with evidence. Tell her that it is a simple equation: if she faces the problem, it will get better; if she doesn't, it will continue to get worse.

Chapter 11

WHAT OUR DAUGHTERS ARE SAYING ABOUT US

WHILE YOU'RE TEACHING your daughter about love, life, and the inevitability of getting your period when you're away for the weekend and have forgotten to pack any Tampax, your daughter has a lot to teach you. Of course she can clue you in about what it's like to be a teenager, let you listen to her favorite CD, help you throw away your most embarrassing wardrobe losers. But the most important thing you can learn from her is something about yourself.

Mothers are a main topic of conversation for your daughter and her friends. Adolescent girls bond because of shared interests and shared mother experiences. "I hate my mother too," one girl says to another, and all of a sudden they have a lot in common. Two girls complaining about their mothers turn to another girl and say, "You have a wonderful mother, you wouldn't understand." They compare notes: "You're so lucky that your mother lets you do that. Mine would *kill* me," or, "What's with your mother? She treats you like a baby."

Why is it that a girl who will barely talk *to* her mother will have no problem talking endlessly *about* her? The power and importance of mothers comes up over and over. Your smallest comments, even those from years ago, are seared into her memory. Why is it that your daughter, who one-on-one finds you beyond dull, seems to feel you're a fascinating creature when she's with her friends? Don't get too flattered. Mostly it's because talking about her mother helps an adolescent girl process her feelings. A girl needs to understand who her mother is—what kind of woman, what kind of mother—and what makes her tick. Once she does, she can consolidate her own identity and successfully separate. She can come to terms with the voice of her mother that's in her head and find her own voice.

The more you understand how hard she's working on creating her identity, the more you can tolerate what she's saying about you (sometimes her criticism is brutal) and the more you can support her.

We took a survey of five hundred girls from all over the country and interviewed many others by e-mail. We also met with girls in several cities around the country and consulted with professionals such as Dr. Sheila Reindl, author of *Sensing the Self*, who are on the front lines in dealing with girls who are dealing with body image issues and eating disorders. Dr. Reindl observed: "The idea of listening to our daughters assumes that mothers need to begin with curiosity, with a real openness and willingness to see things from their perspective and learn from them. This strikes me as being itself a gem of an idea that we, in turn, can offer them."

Dr. Reindl asked a group of girls with eating disorders what advice they would give their mothers. In their discussion of the issues they would like to share, these girls talked about the connection between body image and what went on at the family dinner table. They mentioned the difficulties of living in a house where their father ate everything and their mother was constantly dieting. A couple of girls said that their mothers would often make the family meal but not eat any of it. They talked about the importance of role models (mothers and fathers who ate well, exercised, had a healthy perspective, and didn't obsess about weight). And they brought up the fact that health concerns and body image concerns got confused and entangled for them at home.

In our survey we asked girls aged fourteen to nineteen the same kinds of questions about their body image issues in relationship to their mothers. Most of the girls were amazingly responsive, confirming our thesis that this is a hot, hot topic for girls. They commented on their mothers' constant worry about body weight and their never-ending nutrition advice. They objected to scary warnings about family traits and a genetic predisposition to obesity, which their mothers informed them would surely lead to disappointments in life and love. Mothers who gave backhanded compliments ("Honey, you look fine, it's just that your butt's getting too big and you need to watch it!") got lots of critical comments. Some girls said that when their mothers said *nothing* to them about body image issues, they felt frustrated and assumed that their mothers were withholding their real feelings, when in reality, the mothers may have been just trying *not* to reinforce their daughters' preoccupation with body image.

No wonder mothers and daughters find it hard to talk at all. We have selected some typical survey responses as well as some priceless comments that these girls shared with us. Here are our questions and the answers that the girls gave us, along with our comments or interpretations. Listen to what these girls are saying and see if you can identify with the mothers they describe.

QUESTION: WHAT DOES YOUR MOTHER SAY ABOUT YOUR BODY AND WEIGHT ISSUES THAT DRIVES YOU CRAZY?

Silence is* not *golden.

Age 18, MD: She doesn't say anything—and that drives me crazy!

Age 19, KY: She does not comment to me about my body or weight.

Age 14, NY: What my mother says about body issues doesn't bother me. We don't talk about it; actually, we don't usually talk at all.

Her mother gives her double messages.

Age 15, NY: She tells me to eat more, then she tells me to watch out and not eat so much or I'll get fat . . . I don't know what she wants me to do. She says one thing, then the opposite. It's the kind of thing she's always doing that drives me nuts.

Age 19, IL: She constantly nags me over how "fat" I am and then reverses her opinion when I tell her that I want to go on a diet.

Age 17, WA: She tells me I look fine, when I know for a fact that I don't. Then, if I'm eating something fattening, she tells me that I won't be able to fit into jeans that I just bought.

Age 17, OH: She constantly tells me that I don't need to lose weight and that dieting is unhealthy. Then she goes on yo-yo diets all the time herself.

Age 18, AZ: "If you want to lose weight, eat less." Then, "You aren't eating enough, eat more. You're not that bad."

Age 19, CA: She says how I used to be really skinny but now I'm fat, and because I'm fat, I've become shorter than I was when I was skinny, because the fat weighs me down.

Age 16, NH: That she loves me for who I am, not what I look like, but I could stand to lose a few inches.

Sometimes the message is loud and clear.

Age 19, MD: My mom drives me nuts about my weight because it's all my family cares about. My mom says she didn't get fat until she was pregnant, but I on the other hand just have a bad metabolism. She always makes me feel like I am so fat, and so not a part of the family body types. Also, she is constantly commenting on how if I lost weight, I could wear different clothing and feel better when dressing up.

Age 17, NY: My mom gets mad at me for being a vegetarian. She thinks I just do it to get attention.

Age 19, VA: "How long have you had that pimple?"

Age 19, TX: I am very overweight and I would never get a man worth having because of my weight. She says my weight is something that holds me back from the real world and is the cause of any problems in my life that arise.

Try to comfort her, and she feels uncomfortable.

Age 15, NY: She tells me that I'm bigger because of muscles—I play soccer—but I think she's just trying to make me feel better about my fat thighs.

Age 14, NY: She tells me I'll feel better if I stand up straight, eat properly, and exercise. I do these things, but she never thinks I do, and then I get insulted because she thinks I don't try hard enough.

Age 15, LA: My mom always tells me that I look great. But every once in a while when she says something critical, it makes it so much worse. When she tells me I look fat, I know that I should try and exercise and eat a little healthier, but sometimes it's hard for me and then I just feel guilty.

Whose body is it?

Age 17, PA: My mother says that I have a nice body, although she believes that I shouldn't show it off. She objects to any skintight clothes, low-cut T-shirts, etc., that I wear. She also tells me I should wear makeup so I would look nicer, but it's too time-consuming and it gives me zits.

Age 16, DE: My mom and I both have a problem with our weight, so she thinks she knows how I feel, but sometimes I want her to know that my problems are different from hers.

Age 16, CA: My mom is always bugging me about not snacking so much and eating healthy. She says I'll gain weight even though I work out every day and I play team sports. It ends up getting me really self-conscious. I don't get how criticizing the way I eat will make me want to lose weight; it just gets me more depressed and unfortunately I eat more.

Age 18, NC: She suggests diet programs, she gets me memberships at the gym, and she bugs me about changes in my appearance that I could make. I resent the implication that I need to lose weight, and it bothers me that she places so much importance on how I look.

Age 19, NY: She wants me to eat healthier. She doesn't like me eating processed foods and she wants me to take a *million* multivitamins a day.

Age 18, OH: She always picks on me and teases me about gaining weight.

Age 17, TN: She says I need to eat more, gain weight, stop exercising, 'cause I'm too skinny.

Age 16, PA: She compares my body and weight to hers, saying they are similar. I don't want to be told that I have the body of my mother.

Age 18, PA: She tells me that I'm fat and says I will get to be like my father's side of the family—obese.

Who's controlling her now?

Age 17, VA: She's always telling me to diet and not eat certain things. I hate that.

Age 18, IL: She always tells me if I want to lose weight,

she'll help me. But all the help amounts to is her saying, "Do you think you should be eating that?" or, "Do you need that?"

Age 16, MI: My mom has a weight problem and sometimes she tells me to watch what I eat or else I'll have the same problem she does. She makes me feel like I'm constantly being watched to make sure I'm not "overdoing" it when I eat.

Age 15, IN: She is always telling me I'm gonna end up fat just like her, no matter what, 'cause it's in my jeans [genes?].

Age 16, TX: She tries to scare me by warning me that being overweight is dangerous. It could lead to diabetes, which runs in our family, and it can hold me back from being successful in the real world. She thinks it's the cause of all of my problems. I think this isn't helping me to feel better.

It's a competition.

Age 19, WI: When my sister and I were younger, my mom would always say don't eat this or that because it will make you fat. She would constantly compare us. She still tells me that I need to watch my figure because no man will want me if I'm not thin.

Age 17, MO: My mom always talks about how thin I am and how fat she is. I have my flaws and she makes it sound as if I'm a supermodel. Besides, she's not that fat!

Age 18, MD: She keeps saying that she never had a stomach at all when she was young.

Age 16, CT: "You know, you don't have your sister's body, you should really watch what you eat. Are you really going to eat all of that?!"

Age 16, CA: She says she wishes my breasts were bigger. I'm a 34A. She says she was a stick figure at my age so I'm much better off than she was, so she thinks I don't have much to complain about.

Age 18, OH: "I guess you'll never fit into my wedding dress." *Grrrr.*

QUESTION: IF YOU COULD TELL YOUR MOTHER SOMETHING ABOUT HOW SHE RELATES TO YOUR BODY IMAGE ISSUES, WHAT WOULD YOU TELL HER?

This hits a nerve.

Age 17, WI: I would tell my mother to stop commenting on things I never asked her opinion on, such as my clothes (too tight or too small) or the number of calories in something that I'm eating as a way to discourage me from eating it.

Age 16, TX: I would tell her to leave me alone and *not* point out the obvious!

Age 18, CA: I would tell her that I like the way I look and that when she tells me that I'm as skinny as a pole, it hurts my feelings.

Age 15, NY: "Mom, you haven't seen me naked in a long time."

Age 18, FL: I would tell her that I wish she'd be more accepting of the way my body looks. That not everyone can be so self-controlled like she is about her weight. Her comments sometimes hurt me, and I know that she doesn't realize that I take her comments seriously.

Age 16, IN: I'm fairly thin and as long as I'm happy, she shouldn't say anything to me. It's not wrong to weigh 120. I would like her to give me positive feedback about how I look all of the time instead of telling me that I should work out more.

Age 16, FL: I would tell her to stop trying to "help" me lose weight, because it doesn't really help very much.

Age 18, IL: I would tell her that just because she's my mom, she says things that may not be the truth, and that I don't want to hear little lies about how I look.

Age 17, CA: My mother yells at me and forces me to eat when I get depressed, and I've had an eating disorder in the past. I know that she doesn't mean to insult me at all, she's just regurgitating everything that society tells all women. It angers me that she thinks I'm not up to my full potential. She reassures me that she means well and loves me, but it doesn't help when she gets pissed at me.

QUESTION: DOES YOUR MOTHER HAVE HER OWN BODY IMAGE ISSUES?

Age 15, NY: She watches her weight and everything she eats. She makes a big deal out of everything.

Age 19, NV: She struggles trying to keep her own weight down and she's never happy with how she looks.

Age 16, PA: My mom thinks she's fat. In our house, even the dog is on a diet.

Age 15, CO: She wants to lose weight, but she tends to accept her body more than I accept mine.

Age 18, NH: Our genetic makeup is naturally heavy, but my mother feels compulsive about being thin. She looks at the rest of the world and compares herself, even though there's not that much she can do about it.

Age 14, VT: She says we're not mammoths, we're just husky.

QUESTION: DOES SHE THINK THAT YOU HAVE THE SAME PROBLEM? OR DOES SHE THINK THAT YOU'RE LUCKY, BECAUSE YOU DON'T?

Age 18, PA: Sometimes I think her body image issues feed into mine. Maybe if she had a better body image, it would rub off on me . . . because she has a really great figure and she never seems satisfied, and that sort of gets to me because I wonder, if she thinks *her* body isn't good enough, then maybe mine isn't good either.

Age 17, KY: My mother thinks I have the same problem as she does, even though she's twice my size. She doesn't really have a clear picture of herself!

Age 16, OK: She doesn't think that we have the same problem, but she thinks that her nagging will prevent me from getting any excess weight in the future.

Age 16, FL: She thinks I'm lucky. She doesn't realize that I work hard to keep my weight down.

Age 17, NJ: She thinks I do have the same problem . . . which I know I do, and I don't need a constant reminder.

QUESTION: DOES SHE WORRY ABOUT YOU DIETING? DOES SHE WORRY IF YOU'RE TOO FAT OR TOO THIN?

Age 16, IL: She worries about my becoming obsessed with being thin.

Age 18, KS: She's very two-sided. If I'm worrying about my weight, she'll tell me it's not good to be too thin. But if I'm eating more of something than she thinks I should, she reminds me that I'll get fat.

Age 17, NJ: I think my mother would worry *if* I dieted. She always likes to make sure I'm well fed. She's very motherly that way.

Age 14, MI: She worries if I gain five pounds.

Age 16, LA: She never comments when I lose weight, she says I'm "just fine." But when I say I'm trying to live a more healthy lifestyle, she gets all excited.

Age 14, CA: She wants me to go to a doctor because she worries that I'm too skinny and diet too much.

QUESTION: DOES YOUR MOTHER RESPECT YOUR PRIVACY?

Age 15, NY: I don't have to worry about privacy. My mother respects my privacy because she's never home.

Age 17, TX: She constantly talks about me and what I'm doing with her friends and other people. I don't understand it. Doesn't she realize it's none of their business what I do?

Age 16, TN: She "cleans" my room when it doesn't need to be because she thinks it's a good cover for snooping. I tell her a lot of stuff, so this gets annoying, because I feel as if she needs to make a choice: we can either be friends and I can tell her stuff, or she can be the type of mom who just sneaks around to find stuff out about me and then I won't talk to her, but it can't be both.

Age 17, CT: My mother goes back and forth. When I keep a diary, she never reads it, and she won't open my mail. But if I've already opened my mail and left it in my room, she will look through my things and then question me about it.

Age 16, SC: She pretends to respect my privacy, but she snoops around all the time.

Age 16, WA: She hardly gives me any privacy and it drives me nuts. If I have something important to tell a friend, I have to do it in school or call on my cell phone. I password protect my computer.

Age 18, PA: She pretty much respects my privacy. She's learned to keep out of my business unless I ask her to help me. It's much better if I tell her what's going on.

Age 19, NY: Sometimes she's curious, but she respects my privacy.

Age 16, KY: My mother stays out of my room and doesn't pry into my life. I share most things with her, so she doesn't feel the need to go snooping around.

Age 17, TN: She doesn't respect my privacy. She has listened in on my phone calls and read private letters. I wish she would realize that I need privacy, and that I do know what I'm doing even if she disagrees with my actions.

Age 16, SD: My mom is like any other parent. She trusts me to a certain degree, she tries to respect my privacy, but sometimes her curiosity overcomes that respect!

QUESTION: DO YOU FEEL THAT YOU CAN TELL YOUR MOTHER PERSONAL THINGS?

Yes, no, maybe, I can't.

Age 17, LA: I tell her about things that are necessary, but I think I talk extensively about some aspects of my life and not at all about other parts.

Age 18, MI: Yes, I talk to her about a lot of things. She's my main adviser in life.

Age 17, PA: It really depends on the issue. I can tell her certain personal things like school and sports, but not boyfriends and parties because she would bug me about it.

Age 18, MD: No. I have not told her anything personal except whenever I have my period. I didn't even tell her that I have had sex . . . God knows, she wouldn't go for that.

Age 17, CA: Definitely. Out of all us kids, me and her are probably the closest. Sometimes I feel she doesn't tell me things because she doesn't want me to worry.

QUESTIONS: IF THERE WAS ONE THING YOU WOULD LIKE YOUR MOTHER TO REALIZE ABOUT YOU, WHAT WOULD IT BE?

Age 18, CA: That I'm not as negative and moody as I often appear to her. Being my mother, she gets to hear all of the complaining. I would never be as cranky and rude around my friends as I sometimes am around my mother.

Age 18, KS: I am a woman now. She has taught me well, but there are some things I have to learn on my own.

Age 18, NC: I'm not a baby anymore and that I am a grown-up. I am going to have to make choices for myself and not have someone constantly tell me, "Be careful, don't do this or that."

Age 17, CO: I am more breakable than she thinks.

Age 17, NY: That she has done a good job raising me, so that I am ready to face the world with more independence. Just because I'm going to college doesn't mean our lives and our relationship will diverge.

Age 19, FL: I would like her to realize that I'm a hard worker and I love her and that's enough.

Age 17, DE: That I'm my own person and that just because my opinion is different than hers, that doesn't make it automatically wrong.

Age 16, NH: That I love her for who she is now and not just because she's my mom.

Age 19, OH: That I wish she talked to me about more personal things. She asks too few questions about my personal life.

Age 17, TX: That I'm not good or bad based on my weight.

Age 17, MI: I have done a lot of bad things in the past, but I'm improving myself, and even though there were some bad things in the past, I wouldn't go back and change anything, because it has helped to shape the person I am today and will be in the future.

Age 17, TN: I'm not going to be perfect, and she can't live her life through me.

Age 16, CA: I'm a lot like her and I'm going to make some mistakes and she should just be able to support me in that.

Age 19, MI: I have a lot more anger inside me than she knows. We went through a lot together in high school, but she never asked me about anything. I feel like she didn't know me and it still hurts even now. I want our relationship to get better.

Age 16, IL: I want her to quit worrying about me, I'm not a little girl anymore.

Age 19, DC: It's hard to feel like I'm old and then be treated like a child.

Age 16, CT: I'm not as young as she thinks, so let me have my freedom, but still protect me and love me and snuggle with me.

Ahhhh

Age 15, CA: That I love her more than she will ever know.

RESOURCES

ORGANIZATIONS SERVING TEENAGE GIRLS AND PARENTS

Health, Mental Health, and Eating Disorders

American Anorexia/Bulimia
Association, Inc.
165 West 46th Street
New York, NY 10036
(212) 575-6200
www.nationaleatingdisorders.org

Anxiety Disorders Association
of America (ADAA)
11900 Parklawn Drive, Suite 100
Rockville, MD 20852
(301) 231-9350
www.adaa.org

Eating Disorders Association
0845 634 7650
www.edauk.com

MIND Infoline
0845 766 0163
www.mind.org.uk

Parentline
0808 800 2222
www.parentlineplus.org.uk

The Samaritans
10 The Grove, Slough,
Berks SL1 1QP
01753 216500

Society for Adolescent Medicine
1916 NW Copper Oaks Circle
Blue Springs, MO 64015
(816) 224-8010
www.adolescenthealth.org

Drug and Alcohol Use

ALATEEN
*teen services of Alcoholics
Anonymous*
0207 403 0888
www.alcoholics-
anonymous.org.uk

Drug Information on the Internet
www.clubdrugs.org

GIRL POWER!
U.S. Department of Health and
Human Services
www.health.org/gpower

Narcotics Anonymous
National Helpline
0207 730 0009

National Drugs Helpline
0800 776600

Runaways

National Missing Persons
Helpline
0500 700 700

National Runaway Hotline
1-800-231-6946

Sexuality

FPA's Contraception Helpline
0845 310 1344
www.fpa.org.uk

Lesbian and Gay Switchboard
0207 837 7324

National AIDS Helpline
0800 567 123

National Campaign to Prevent
Teen Pregnancy
2100 M Street NW
Washington, DC 20037
(202) 331-7735
www.teenpregnancy.org

National STD Hotline
1-800-227-8922
www.ashastd.org

Parents and Friends of Lesbians
and Gays (PFLAG)
1101 Fourteenth Street NW,
Suite 1030
Washington, DC 20005
(202) 638-4200
www.info@pflag.org

Planet Out
for gay and lesbian youth
www.planetout.com

Planned Parenthood
Federation of America
810 Seventh Avenue
New York, NY 10019
1-800-230-PLAN
www.plannedparenthood.org

Rape, Abuse, Incest National
Network (RAINN)
free confidential counseling
1-800-656-HOPE
www.rainn.org

Rape Crisis
0207 837 1600

Self-Harm

S.A.F.E. (Self-Abuse Finally Ends)
639 Dundas Street
London, Ontario
Canada, N5W 2Z1

SAFE Alternatives at Rock
Creek Center
1-800-DONTCUT

SelfHarm.Com
www.selfharm.com

Web site on self-injury
www.palace.net/~llama/selfinjury

YWCA
01865 304 200
www.ywca-gb.org.uk

Sports

Women's Sports Foundation
Eisenhower Park
East Meadow, NY 11554
e-mail: wosport@aol.com
www.womenssportsfoundation.org

RESOURCES ON THE INTERNET

www.daughters.com
a newsletter for parents of girls

www.dadsanddaughters.org

sxetc.org
*a sex education Web site and forum
from Rutgers University*

www.something-fishy.com
a comprehensive eating disorders site

www.hedc.org
Harvard Eating Disorders
Center

www.about-face.org
*a media literacy organization
focusing on the impact of
media on body image*

www.adiosbarbie.com
a positive body image site

nm-server.jrn.columbia.edu/
projects/masters/bodyimage
*"body (i)con," a new media project
from Columbia University*

www.feminist.com

www.gurl.com

www.now.org
National Organization for
Women

www.andreasvoice.org
on eating disorders

www.goaskalice.columbia.edu
Columbia University's Health
Education Program

www.healthyweight.net
Healthy Weight Network

A READING LIST FOR BOTH OF YOU

Bartle, Nathalie, *Venus in Blue Jeans*, Dell

Bordo, Susan, *Unbearable Weight*, University of California Press

Brumberg, Joan Jacobs, *The Body Project*, Vintage Books

———, *Fasting Girls*, Vintage Books

Dudman, Martha, *Augusta, Gone*, Simon & Schuster

Edelman, Hope, *Motherless Daughters*, Dell

Fallon, P., S. Wooley, and M. Katzman, editors, *Feminist Perspectives on Eating Disorders*, Guilford Press

Hirschmann, Jane, and Lela Zaphiropoulos, *Preventing Childhood Eating Problems*, Gurze Books

Hornbacher, Marya, *Wasted*, HarperCollins

Lamott, Anne, *Traveling Mercies*, Anchor Books

Levenkron, Steven, *The Best Little Girl in the World*, Warner Books

———, *Cutting*, Warner Books

———, *The Luckiest Girl in the World*, Warner Books

Lopez, Ralph, M.D. *The Teen Health Book: A Parents' Guide to Adolescent Health and Well-Being*, Norton

Madaras, Lynda, *The What's Happening to My Body? Book for Girls*, Newmarket Press

Maine, Margo, Ph.D., *Father Hunger*, Gurze Books

Marks, Andrea, M.D., and Betty Rothbart, M.S.W., *Healthy Teens, Body and Soul: A Parent's Complete Guide to Adolescent Health*, Simon & Schuster

Marone, Nicky, *How to Father a Successful Daughter*, Fawcett

Pipher, Mary, *Reviving Ophelia*, Ballantine Books

Ponton, Lynn E., *The Sex Lives of Teenagers: Revealing the Secret World of Adolescent Boys and Girls*, Plume

Reindl, Sheila, *Sensing the Self: Women's Recovery from Bulimia*, Harvard University Press

Tanenbaum, Leora, *Slut!*, Perennial

Tannen, Deborah, *I Only Say This Because I Love You*, Random House

Wolf, Anthony E., *Get Out of My Life, but First Could You Drive Me and Cheryl to the Mall?: A Parent's Guide to the New Teenager*, Noonday Press

Wolf, Naomi, *The Beauty Myth*, Anchor

——, *Promiscuities*, Fawcett Books

Wurtzel, Elizabeth, *Prozac Nation*, Riverhead Books

Zerbe, Kathryn, M.D., *The Body Betrayed*, Gurze Books

P.S.

IN THE FINAL EPISODE of MTV's popular show *Daria*, the title character gives her high school commencement address and offers the following advice:

> Stand firm for what you believe in until or unless logic and experience prove you wrong. Remember, when the emperor looks naked, the emperor *is* naked. The truth and a lie are not sort of the same thing. And there's no aspect, no facet, no moment of life that can't be improved with pizza.

From Pablo Casals (1971)

> You are a marvel.
> Each second we live is a new and unique moment of the
>   universe,
> A moment that will never be again . . .
> And what do we teach our children?
>
> We teach them that two and two make four, and that Paris
>   is the capital of France. When will we also teach them
>   what they are?

We should say to each of them:

Do you know what you are? You are a marvel.
You are unique. In all the years that have passed, there has
never been another child like you. Your legs, your arms,
your clever fingers, the way you move.

You may become a Shakespeare, a Michelangelo, a
Beethoven.
You have the capacity for anything.
Yes, you are a marvel. And when you grow up, can you
then harm another who is, like you, a marvel?

You must work—we all must work—to make the world
worthy of its children.

INDEX

abuse, 8, 30, 104, 206–7, 211, 232.
See also substance abuse
accident-proneness, 194
acting out
    and commonly experienced
      emotional problems, 194
    and father-daughter relation-
      ships, 109, 120
    and food and nutrition, 144
    and how and when to
      intervene, 183
    and mother-daughter relation-
      ships, 63
    and sex/sexuality, 165, 212
acute stress disorders, 187
addictions, 84, 171–172, 192, 195,
    198, 202
alcohol, 86, 104, 173–74, 194,
    212, 231–32
alienation, 13, 37, 96, 101. *See also*
    isolation
Andreavoice.org, 145
anorexia, 2, 5, 145, 197–198,
    200
anxiety
    and archetypes of mothers,
      95–98
    and battles of body ownership,
      23
    and body image basics, 11, 16
    as disorder, 185–190
    and eating disorders, 188, 204
    of fathers, 115

    and issues facing daughters and
      mothers, 181
    and mother-daughter relation-
      ships, 44, 53, 62, 65
    of mothers, 175
    and sex/sexuality, 166, 175, 212
    and teen pregnancy, 206
archetypes of mothers, 19,
    92–103, 104
attention, getting, 34, 63, 64,
    77–78, 107, 219

bad boys, 169–170
bargaining/negotiating, 41–42,
    139
beauty, stereotypes of, 53, 60–62
The Beauty Myth (Wolf), 61
Big Talks, 82
binge drinking, 172
binge eating, 5, 8, 135, 145, 149,
    197, 200
bipolar disorder, 192
birth control, 180
bisexuality, 208
blame
    and archetypes of mothers, 99,
      100
    and body image issues, 4
    and commonly experienced
      emotional problems, 186,
      187, 190
    and father-daughter relation-
      ships, 110, 118, 121

blame (*cont.*)
   and food and nutrition, 139,
      144
   and how and when to
      intervene, 183, 184
   and mother-daughter relation-
      ships, 7–8, 31, 41, 63–64, 65
   and problems of sexual health,
      210
body
   changes in, 23–26, 164–65
   as means of expressing
      thoughts, feelings, and
      problems
    about sex, 173–174
   ownership of, 11, 21–26,
      220–21
   See also body image
body dismorphic disorder, 189
body image
   anticipating problems about,
      17–18
   basics about, 10–20
   and body as enemy, 142
   daughters's focus on, 10, 11,
      12–15, 21, 24–25, 212–13
   definition of, 5
   and father-daughter relation-
      ships, 16–17, 109, 115–116,
      125
   female peer influence on,
      53–54
   generational influences on,
      52–53
   girls most at risk for negative,
      16–17
   how to help daughters with,
      17–19
   media messages about, 60–62,
      162–163
   and mother-daughter relation-
      ships, 6–7, 10, 11–12, 39

   of mothers, 2, 10, 20, 52,
      59–60, 94, 131, 140–141,
      224–226
   mothers as source of attitudes
      about, 54–55
   mother's role in helping
      daughters with, 12–18
   pervasiveness of concern about,
      2, 3, 4, 5–6
   questions about, 3–4
   reasons for problems
      concerning, 5–6
   resources about, 233
   unconscious/unspoken
      messages about, 52–53
   and what daughters say about
      mothers, 217, 218–223,
      224–226
   what every mother needs to
      know about, 19–20
   See also specific topic
body language, 75
body mass index (BMI), 200
boundaries
   and archetypes of mothers,
      94
   and battles of body ownership,
      22–23
   and communication between
      mother and daughter, 70
   and eating problems, 203
   and father-daughter relation-
      ships, 113
   and husband-wife relationship,
      106
   and mother-daughter relation-
      ships, 8, 30, 46, 56, 59
   mothers not respecting
      daughter's, 67–68
   and sex/sexuality, 167,
      172–173
   See also setting limits

boyfriends
    acceptance of disrespectful
        treatment from, 212
    breaking up with, 212
    and dating violence, 205
    and father-daughter relation-
        ships, 127, 129
    and problems of sexual health,
        212
    and what daughters say about
        mothers, 228
breakfasts, 148–149
bribery, 67, 155, 184
bulimia, 5, 145, 197–198, 200

Casals, Pablo, 237
chat rooms, internet, 207–208
childhood dreams, 13, 15
Cohen, Phyllis, 4–5
collusion, mother-daughter, 95,
    108
Columbia University, 213
communication, 69–91
    and battles of body ownership,
        26
    and Big Talks, 82
    and body image basics, 19
    body language as, 75
    and conversation as negotia-
        tions, 78
    as conversations or ambushes,
        82–84
    cross-, 71, 80
    about difficult issues, 83–84
    of double messages, 218–219
    and ending conversations, 81
    false, 72–73
    of generational messages, 52–53
    and giving positive feedback,
        74–75
    and humor, 82

    importance of, 87–88
    and killing with kindness, 91
    and lack of answers, 83
    and Landmine Topics, 84–87
    loud and clear, 219–220
    and meaning well and making
        it worse, 90–91
    methods of, 49
    in mother-daughter relation-
        ships, 7, 19, 36–37, 40, 41,
        43, 49, 50, 91
    negative, 63–64
    and negative feedback loop,
        71–72
    principles of, 79–88
    reasons for difficulty in
        mother-daughter, 69–70
    resistence to, 37–38
    about sex/sexuality, 166–167,
        168–169, 173, 175, 177–180
    and speaking the same
        language, 80
    suggested tips for, 78–79
    and talking at daughters, 76–77
    and what daughters say about
        mothers, 218–220, 228,
        230
    and what to say if you never
        want her to talk to you
        again, 89
    See also silence
compensating, 98, 174
competition
    and archetypes of mothers,
        92–93
    and eating disorders, 202
    and food as competitive,
        136–137
    and mother-daughter relation-
        ships, 43, 50, 59, 105–106,
        107, 112, 117, 175–176, 180

competition (*cont.*)
   and sex/sexuality, 163, 175–176, 180
   and what daughters say about mothers, 222–223
complicated bereavement, 192
compliments
   backhanded, 90–91, 217
   bogus, 75
   and communication between mother and daughter, 74–75, 90–91
   and father-daughter relationships, 112–113, 122, 128
   and mother-daughter relationships, 33–34
   and what daughters say about mothers, 217
confidences/confidentiality, 26, 179, 204, 227
confrontation, and helping with acute problems, 214
connection, mother-daughter
   and archetypes of mothers, 103
   and commonly experienced emotional problems, 190
   and communication between mother and daughter, 87
   and food and nutrition, 139
   and mother-daughter relationships, 7, 8, 27, 29, 32–33, 34–35, 39, 48, 58, 59
control
   and archetypes of mothers, 97
   and battles of body ownership, 22, 25
   and body image basics, 11, 12, 18
   and commonly experienced emotional problems, 188, 190

   and communication between mother and daughter, 76
   and dating violence, 205
   and eating disorders, 199–200
   and father-daughter relationships, 113, 115, 121, 126
   and food and nutrition, 76, 132, 133, 137, 139, 142, 144, 157
   guidance as different from, 56–57
   and how and when to intervene, 183
   and internet chat rooms, 207
   and mother-daughter relationships, 35, 41, 45, 48, 56–57, 67
   and sex/sexuality, 173, 207, 209–210
   and what daughters say about mothers, 221–222
counseling, 2, 203, 206
counterphobic mothers, 96
criticism
   and archetypes of mothers, 97–98
   and body image basics, 12, 17–19
   and communication between mother and daughter, 77
   and dating violence, 205
   and eating disorders, 200
   and father-daughter relationships, 16–17, 115, 126, 127
   of mothers by daughters, 12, 40
   self-, 95–96, 135, 202
   and what daughters say about mothers, 220, 221, 222
cutting, 181, 188, 193, 196–197

Daria (MTV show), 237
dating, 172–173, 181, 204–205

daughters
  acting as sons, 107–108, 116
  as babies, 54–55
  comparison to siblings of, 41
  idealization of mothers by, 12, 13
  issues facing, 181
  as princesses, 116
  remaking, 56, 57
  responsibilities of, 38
  as source of pleasure for mothers, 55
  unreasonable behavior of, 36–38
  and what daughters would tell mothers, 222–223
  and what they say about mothers, 215–232
  as work in progress, 77
  See also specific topic
death of mothers, 209
defensiveness, 40, 64, 144, 171, 205, 211, 214
delinquency, 192
denial, 53, 115, 181, 184, 190, 203, 213
depression
  and archetypes of mothers, 102
  and body image basics, 17, 18
  and commonly experienced emotional problems, 190–194
  and cutting, 196
  as deceptive, 193
  and eating disorders, 201, 202, 204
  and food and nutrition, 143, 158
  forms of, 191–192
  and genetics, 191
  as issue facing daughters, 181

  misdiagnosis of, 192
  and mother-daughter relationships, 36, 39
  and sex/sexuality, 171, 191
  signs/symptoms of, 191, 192–194
  and suicide, 195
  and teen pregnancy, 206
  and what daughters say about mothers, 221, 223
  and when to intervene, 190–94, 196
dieting
  and battles of body ownership, 24
  and dating violence, 205
  and depression, 143
  as disordered eating, 197
  and eating disorders, 199, 200
  fad, 146, 155
  and fat as failure, 143–144
  and food as competitive, 136–137
  and food as feeling that doesn't feel good, 137–138
  making sense of, 156–157
  and mother-daughter relationships, 8
  of mothers, 217, 219
  mothers' worries about, 226
  obsession with, 130
  psychological effects of, 157
  and use of food to attain goals, 132
  and what daughters say about mothers, 217, 219, 221, 226
  See also eating; food; nutrition
disordered eating
  eating disorders distinguished from, 144–145, 154
  examples of, 197

disordered eating (*cont.*)
   and food as power struggle, 133
   and food as something
      someone else should worry
      about, 139
   and sex/sexuality, 171
   signs of, 145, 160–161
   and when to intervene, 190
distancing, 28–29, 40, 73, 99, 117,
   211
doctors, 184, 203, 204
double standard, 163
dreams, childhood, 13, 15
drug treatment centers, 214
drugs, 8, 86, 104, 183, 185, 194,
   200, 212, 231–32
dual diagnosis, 192
dysthymia, 191

eating
   all-day, 133
   and body image basics, 17
   and commonly experienced
      emotional problems, 193
   and communication between
      mother and daughter, 75–76
   consequences of poor, 138–139,
      157–58
   frequently asked questions
      about, 153–159
   and how to eat, 143
   isolated/secret, 133, 135–136,
      137, 201
   mother's role concerning,
      139–148
   and need for healthy diet,
      150–151
   need for regular, 149–151
   "normal," 153–154
   realistic attitudes about, 147–148
   and what daughters say about
      mothers, 221

   See also disordered eating; eating
      disorders; family meals
eating disorders
   and anxiety, 188, 204
   and body image issues, 5,
      199–200
   causes and characteristics of, 1,
      2, 145, 160, 188,
      198–199, 201–202
   common factors in girls who
      develop, 199–200
   and commonly experienced
      emotional problems,
      197–204
   cure for, 198
   definition of, 197
   and depression, 201, 202, 204
   disordered eating as different
      from, 144–145, 154
   and drugs, 198
   education about, 203
   and family issues, 199
   family members with, 202
   and father-daughter relation-
      ships, 117, 199
   and food and nutrition, 135,
      137, 144–145
   and genetics, 199
   girls at risk for, 202–203
   as issue facing daughters, 181
   and messages from mothers,
      199
   and mother-daughter relation-
      ships, 39
   and peer pressures, 156
   resources about, 231, 233
   and sex/sexuality, 203, 207
   treatments for, 1–2
   triggering of, 144
   and vegetarianism, 153
   ways to help with, 145–146,
      203–204

and what daughters say about mothers, 217, 223

See also anorexia; binge eating; bulimia

emergency rooms, 213

empathy, 26, 29, 30, 31, 32, 76–77, 85, 96, 124, 155

experimentation/exploration, 14, 49, 63, 177, 206, 208

family
    daughters' role in, 37
    and eating disorders, 199, 204
    history of sexual abuse in, 209
    problems of, 182–183, 199, 203, 204, 206
    and problems of sexual health, 208–209
    and teen pregnancy, 206

family meals, 133, 202, 217

fashions
    and battles of body ownership, 24
    and father-daughter relationships, 112–115, 125, 126–127
    and what daughters say about mothers, 220, 222

fat
    and battles of body ownership, 24
    and eating disorders, 199, 200
    food as equal to, 76, 132, 134, 137, 143–144, 158
    importance in diet of, 148, 151
    meaning of, 75
    and problems of sexual health, 208
    unspoken messages about, 53
    and what daughters say about mothers, 218, 219, 220, 221, 222, 226

what every mother needs to know about, 19

fathers, 104–129
    abdication of responsibilities by, 123
    antagonism toward/denigration of, 108, 109, 118, 119
    anxiety of, 115
    as authority figure, 110
    and basic dynamics of adolescence, 112–113
    and body image basics, 16–17
    confusion and hurt of, 108–109, 110–111, 112
    and eating disorders, 117, 199
    fashion opinions of, 112–115, 125, 126–127
    as "good time" guy, 120–121
    as heavies, 46, 121
    as in loop, 123–124
    and mother-daughter relationships, 41, 46–47
    and Oedipal process, 105–106, 107, 112, 117
    pushing away/ignoring of, 107, 116–117, 118, 119, 120, 123
    putting down of women by, 127
    reality check for, 124
    as role models, 106–107
    role of, 104–105, 107, 108–109, 110, 124–125, 127, 128
    and sex/sexuality, 167, 180
    as single parents, 106–107, 120, 128
    taking risks by, 123
    as threatened, 115
    and what daughters say about mothers, 217
    withdrawal of, 111

See also relationships, father-daughter

feedback, 25, 71–72, 74–75
flirting, and father-daughter relationships, 109, 116, 126
food
    bargains about, 139
    as comfort, 143
    as competitive, 136–137
    and eating as negative experience, 132
    as embarrassing, 136
    as enemy, 134
    fat as equal to, 76, 132, 134, 137, 143–144
    as feeling that doesn't feel good, 137–138
    frequently asked questions about, 153–159
    and guidelines for feeding and nourishing daughters, 148–153
    as language everyone but you speaks, 135
    mother's role concerning, 139–148
    mothers' attitudes about, 140–141, 146–147
    and need for healthy diet, 150–151
    and not taking daughters seriously, 140
    and peer pressures, 155–156
    as pleasure, 147
    as power struggle, 133
    as scary, 137
    signs of problems related to, 158–159
    social aspects of, 133
    as something someone else should worry about, 138–139
    use of, to attain goals, 132
    as working magically, 134

    See also family meals
food quirks, 201
friends
    and battles of body ownership, 26
    and body image basics, 17, 20
    comparison with, 26
    disparagement of, 146
    and food as competitive, 136
    influence of, 42, 43
    loss of, 17
    mother and daughter as best, 38–39
    as mother substitutes, 135
    and sex/sexuality, 163
    and what daughters say about mothers, 215
    See also peers

gender issues, 121–122, 195–196, 208. See also homosexuality
generalized anxiety disorders, 185, 186–187
generational experiences, 25, 52–53, 59. See also genetics
genetics, 90, 191, 199, 217, 219, 222, 225. See also generational experiences
goaskalice.columbia.edu, 213
guidance
    control as different from, 56–57
    in mother-daughter relationships, 56, 57, 58, 63, 65
guilt
    and body image issues, 2
    and commonly experienced emotional problems, 194
    and food and nutrition, 139, 141
    and mother-daughter relationships, 7–8, 39, 40, 41

and problems of sexual health, 212

and what daughters say about mothers, 220

help, resistance to, 37–38, 213, 214

homophobia, 209

homosexuality, 168–169, 170–71, 197, 208, 210, 211, 232

honesty, and how and when to intervene, 184

"hooking up," 206–207

hover/smother mothers, 19, 96–97

humor, 30, 33, 48, 82

husbands, 104–129
  and mother's role in father-daughter relationships, 111–112, 118–124
  wife's relationship with, 106, 107–108, 118–120
  See also fathers

hypervigilant mothers, 181–182

hypochondria, 194

identity issues
  and body image issues, 6, 16
  and father-daughter relationships, 104, 112
  and food and nutrition, 143
  and husband-wife relationship, 106
  and mother-daughter relationships, 34–35, 39, 65
  and sex/sexuality, 168
  sexual, 168–69, 204, 207, 208, 209
  and what daughters say about mothers, 216
  and when to intervene, 195
  See also self-image

immune system, 158

incest, 188

Internet, as resource, 3, 233

intervention
  and determining whose problem it is, 182–183
  and how and when to intervene, 181–214
  and how to help with acute problems, 213–214
  and issues facing daughters and mothers, 182
  and mother-daughter relationships, 36–37, 49
  and problems of sexual health, 212
  resistance to, 37–38, 184, 213, 214

intrusion. See intervention

isolation, 17, 18, 201, 205. See also alienation

Just Because Age, 73

Kaiser Family Foundation, 205

killing with kindness, 91

Landmine Topics, 84–87

lesbianism, 168–169, 208

Levine, Kathy, 152

listening
  and archetypes of mothers, 102
  and battles of body ownership, 25
  and body image basics, 19
  and communication between mother and daughter, 77–78, 85
  and how to help with acute problems, 214
  and mother-daughter relationships, 7, 27, 37, 39–40, 43, 48, 62–63, 64

listening (*cont.*)
    selective, 102
    and sex/sexuality, 167, 171, 212
    and what daughters say about
        mothers, 216
Lopez, Ralph, 213
love
    and archetypes of mothers, 98,
        101
    and battles of body ownership,
        24
    and body image issues, 2, 12
    and communication between
        mother and daughter, 70–71
    and eating disorders, 199
    and father-daughter relation-
        ships, 125
    and mother-daughter relation-
        ships, 7, 28, 29, 39, 53,
        54–55, 56, 65
    and sex/sexuality, 171, 177
    and teen pregnancy, 206
    and what daughters say about
        mothers, 219, 223, 229, 230
lying, 202, 211, 223

Madaras, Lynda, 23
manic depression, 192
manipulation, 41, 112, 116, 117,
    127, 184, 211
masturbation, 164, 165
media, 17, 62–64, 164–65, 233
menstruation, 23, 25–26, 148, 164,
    199, 228
mentoring, 116, 175
merged mothers, 93–95
micromanagement, 18, 56, 140,
    155
mistakes, learning from, 56–57
mobile crisis teams, 213
mother figures, 209
"mother hunger," 101

mothers
    adolescence of, 93–95
    archetypes of, 92–103
    body image of, 2, 10, 20, 52, 59–
        60, 94, 131, 140–141, 224–226
    core questions of, 10
    daughters as extension of,
        94–95
    daughters as source of pleasure
        for, 55
    daughters' idealization of, 12, 13
    daughters' understanding of,
        216
    death of, 209
    and father-daughter relation-
        ships, 110, 111–112,
        118–124
    fears of, 167
    friends as substitutes for, 135
    ignorance of, 2, 167
    mistakes of, 40–41, 49
    placating of, 72
    as putting on front, 40
    self-image of, 66
    self-understanding of, 62, 76,
        102–103
    as taking a look at themselves,
        51–68
    as threatened, 77, 101
    as too busy, 139
    what daughters say about,
        215–232
    what daughters would tell,
        222–223
    See also specific type of mother or
        topic

not enough mothers archetype,
    101–102
nutrition, 130–131, 160, 217. *See*
    also eating; food
nutritionists, 184, 203

obesity, 5, 154–155, 200–201, 217, 221

obsessive-compulsive disorders, 185, 188–189

Oedipal process, 105–106, 107, 112, 117

organizations, as resources, 231–33

overidentification, 59, 70

overprotectiveness, 176, 209–210

overreactions, 14, 29, 67, 79, 112, 182, 209

ownership of body, 11, 21–26, 220–221

panic attacks, 185, 187–188

Peck, Amy, 152

peers
  and food and nutrition, 155–156
  and food as language everyone but you speaks, 135
  influence of female, 53–54
  and sex/sexuality, 168
  See also friends

perfection
  and archetypes of mothers, 94, 98, 99, 100
  and body image basics, 13
  and eating disorders, 199, 202
  and food and nutrition, 140, 141
  and husband-wife relationship, 107
  and mother-daughter relationships, 40–41, 56, 65
  and what daughters say about mothers, 232

phobias, 185, 187–188

piercing/tattooing, 24, 42, 84, 169

Pipher, Mary, 3

plastic surgery, 189

pornography, 207, 209

post-traumatic stress disorders (PTSD), 187

potentially explosive issues, 43–48

power struggles
  and archetypes of mothers, 101
  and communication between mother and daughter, 79
  and father-daughter relationships, 112, 120
  food as, 133, 139
  and mother-daughter relationships, 43, 46–48
  and sex/sexuality, 173

pregnancy, 175, 210
  teen, 205–206

privacy
  and battles of body ownership, 23, 26
  and communication between mother and daughter, 70, 72
  and eating disorders, 204
  and mother-daughter relationships, 37
  and sex/sexuality, 167, 178
  and what daughters say about mothers, 226–228, 229

problems
  admitting, 214
  anticipating body image, 17–18
  commonly experienced emotional, 184–214
  determining whose, 182–183
  harping on, 85–86
  hiding of, 184
  how and when to intervene in, 181–214
  how to help with acute, 213–214
  ignoring of, 102, 115–16
  lack of answers to, 50
  Landmine Topics as, 84–87
  sharing of, 86

problems (*cont.*)
  solving of, 65, 84
  warning signs of, 183
  ways to express, 182–183
  See also type of problem
professional help
  and cutting, 197
  and eating disorders, 203
  and food and nutrition, 154,
    155
  and how and when to
    intervene, 184
  and teen pregnancy, 206
  See also type of help
projection of feelings, 16, 67, 86
promiscuity, 8, 102, 163, 192, 194,
  207
prying. *See* intervention
psychiatric hospitals, 214
psychosomatic illness, 194
psychotherapy/psychotherapists,
  4, 184, 189, 191, 195, 203
pushing away
  and battles of body ownership,
    22, 24, 25
  and body image basics, 11
  and communication between
    mother and daughter, 71
  and father-daughter relation-
    ships, 107, 116–117, 118,
    119, 120, 123
  and food and nutrition, 134
  and mother-daughter relation-
    ships, 22, 24, 25, 31–32, 35,
    58, 134
  and sex/sexuality, 164

questions, loaded, 79

rape, 205, 212, 232
Reindl, Sheila, 216–217

relationships, father-daughter
  and body image issues, 16–17,
    109, 115–116, 125
  and boundaries, 113
  and control, 113, 115, 121, 126
  and criticism, 16–17, 115, 126,
    127
  and Daddy's Little Girl, 108
  and daughters acting as sons,
    107–108, 116
  and daughters as not needing
    fathers, 108–109
  and daughters as princess, 116
  and eating disorders, 117, 199
  and fashions, 112–115, 125,
    126–127
  and flirting with fathers, 109,
    116, 126
  as love-hate battle, 110
  and mother-daughter
    conspiring against fathers,
    110
  and mother-daughter relation-
    ships, 105–106, 108, 117, 124
  mothers's role in, 111–112,
    118–124
  resources about, 233
  and sex/sexuality, 17, 109, 112,
    114, 116, 117–118, 120,
    122–123, 126, 167, 180
  silence in, 110
  and what fathers should do,
    128–129
  and what fathers should not say
    or do, 126–127
relationships, mother-daughter
  and battles of body ownership,
    22, 24, 26
  benign stupidity in, 50
  and blame, 7–8, 31, 41, 63–64,
    65

and body image issues, 6–7, 10, 11–12, 39
and boundaries, 8, 30, 46, 56, 59
communication in, 7, 19, 36–37, 40, 41, 43, 49, 50, 91
and comparison of siblings, 41
competition/rivalry in, 43, 50, 59, 105–106, 107, 112, 117, 175–176, 180
and compliments, 33–34
and control, 35, 41, 45, 48, 56–57, 67
and eating disorders, 39
and fathers, 41, 46–47, 105–106, 108, 117, 124
and how to keep process going, 49–50
and how to relate, 6–7
humor in, 30, 33, 48
and mistakes of mothers, 49
and mother-daughter as best friends, 38–39
negotiation/bargaining in, 41–42
persistence in, 35
and potentially explosive issues, 43–48
and power struggles, 43, 46–48
as process, 10, 27–50
questions about, 58–59
and reasons for daughters's unreasonable behavior, 36–38
role of mother in, 8–9
and saying and doing hurtful things, 28–29
and sex/sexuality, 39, 180
silence in, 36–37, 41, 64, 68
testing in, 8, 33, 42–43

and things mothers should not do, 40–42
as two-way street, 38, 48
verbal abuse in, 8, 28
what doesn't work in, 30–31
resistance to help, 37–38, 184, 213, 214
resources, 2–3, 231–33, 234–35
respect
and battles of body ownership, 26
and father-daughter relationships, 115, 120
and mother-daughter relationships, 28, 30, 36, 42, 49
and sex/sexuality, 167, 178
responsibility
legal, 213
taking, for eating disorders, 204
Reviving Ophelia (Pipher), 3
rivalry. *See* competition
role models, 19, 20, 51–52, 58, 61, 65, 106–107, 143, 178, 217
runaways, 216, 232
Rutgers University, 213

saying no, 177
school violence, 181
secretiveness, 203, 211
self-confidence, 5, 54, 105
self-consciousness, 187, 221
self-criticism, 95–96, 135, 202
self-defeating behavior, 185
self-deprecation, 76
self-destructive behaviors, 76, 185, 188, 189. *See also specific behavior*
self-esteem
and body image issues, 4, 5, 20
and commonly experienced emotional problems, 194

self-esteem (*cont.*)
  and eating disorders, 202
  and father-daughter relation-
    ships, 117–118, 124
  and food and nutrition, 132
  and mother-daughter relation-
    ships, 39, 41, 55, 60, 65
  of mothers, 98
  and sex/sexuality, 172, 176
  and teen pregnancy, 206
self-hatred/loathing, 76, 201, 212
self-image
  and archetypes of mothers, 97
  and body image, 5, 13, 15
  and father-daughter relation-
    ships, 104, 117, 125
  and food and nutrition, 141
  and mother-daughter relation-
    ships, 30, 55, 63
  mothers as source of attitudes
    about, 54
  and sex/sexuality, 168
  See also identity issues
self-mutilation, 196, 198–99,
    232–33. *See also* cutting
Sensing the Self (Reindl), 216
sensitivity
  and battles of body ownership,
    25
  and communication between
    mother and daughter, 85
  and father-daughter relation-
    ships, 106
  and mother-daughter relation-
    ships, 39–40, 42
separation
  and archetypes of mothers, 97
  and battles of body ownership,
    21–22, 24
  and body image basics, 11–12,
    15, 16
  and communication between
    mother and daughter, 70,
    74, 88
  and eating disorders, 199
  and expression of problems, 182
  and father-daughter relation-
    ships, 105, 106
  and how and when to
    intervene, 182
  and mother-daughter relation-
    ships, 31, 35, 38–39, 47, 59,
    65
  and what daughters say about
    mothers, 216
setting limits
  and archetypes of mothers, 94,
    96
  and mother-daughter relation-
    ships, 8, 27, 38, 57
  See also boundaries
sex/sexuality, 162–180
  and addictions, 171–172
  anal, 207
  and archetypes of mothers, 102
  and bad boys, 169–170
  and battles of body ownership,
    22
  body as means of expressing
    thoughts, feelings, and
    problems about, 173–174
  and body changes, 164–165
  and body image issues, 17,
    162–180
  and boundaries, 172–173
  and commonly experienced
    emotional problems, 191
  communication about, 84,
    166–167, 168–169, 173, 175,
    177–180
  and competition, 163, 175–176,
    180

and conformity, 174
and control, 173, 207, 209–210
and dating, 172–173
and decoding daughters's
    messages, 168–174
and depression, 171, 191
and disordered eating, 171
double standard for, 163
and eating disorders, 203, 207
education about, 166, 212, 213
experimentation and
    exploration about, 177
and father-daughter relation-
    ships, 17, 109, 112, 114,
    116, 117–118, 120, 122–123,
    126, 167, 180
feelings and fantasies about,
    165–166
girls at risk in their, 208–211
group, 207
guidelines for talking about,
    177–179
and how and when to
    intervene, 183
ignorance about, 164
and internet chat rooms,
    207–208
and love, 171, 177
meaning of, 206–207
and mother-daughter relation-
    ships, 39, 180
and mother's fears, 167
mother's ignorance about, 167
and mothers' attitudes and
    roles, 174–177
negative messages about, 173
obsession about, 210
oral, 207
parents's comfort with own,
    208–209
and peer pressures, 168

and power struggles, 173
precocious, 171
premature, 211
and privacy, 167, 178
and problems of sexual health,
    206–213
real, 207
red flags for problems about,
    211–213
and relationships, 171
resources about, 232, 233
safe, 207
and saying no, 177
and self-image, 168
and self-understanding of
    mothers, 103
and sex education, 166
and shyness of mothers, 176
and touching/affection, 167
and unhealthy sex practices, 211
unprotected, 183, 210
and values and standards, 212
and what daughters say about
    mothers, 228
what not to say about, 178–179,
    180
See also homosexuality;
    pregnancy
sexual abuse, 188, 203, 209
sexual identity, 168–169, 204, 207,
    208, 209
sexual predators, 210
sexually transmitted diseases
    (STDs), 209, 212, 232
shame
    and archetypes of mothers,
        99
    and cutting, 197
    and food and nutrition, 145
    and how and when to intervene,
        183, 184

shame (*cont.*)
    and mother-daughter relation-
        ships, 41, 64, 65
shyness
    and battles of body ownership,
        26
    and body image basics, 16
    and commonly experience
        emotional problems, 187
    and communication between
        mother and daughter, 84
    and father-daughter relation-
        ships, 107, 109, 113
    and mother-daughter relation-
        ships, 36–37
    of mothers, 176
    and sex/sexuality, 176
silence
    and battles of body ownership,
        26

    and communication between
        mother and daughter,
        70–71, 73, 81
    and father-daughter relation-
        ships, 110
    and mother-daughter relation-
        ships, 36–37, 41, 64, 68
    and what daughters say about
        mothers, 217–218, 232
single parents, and father-
        daughter relationships,
        106–107, 120, 128
sleep problems, 158, 186, 193
sons, daughters acting as,
        107–108, 116
sports, resources about, 233
stalking, 210
stress, 104, 185, 187, 188
substance abuse, 8, 84, 171–172,
        210. *See also* alcohol; drugs

suicide, 181, 191, 193, 194,
        195–196, 197
super mothers archetype, 99–101
sxetc.org, 213

tattooing/piercing, 24, 42, 84, 169
The Teen Health Book (Lopez), 213
teen health centers, 184
teen outreach programs, 213–214
teen pregnancy, 207–8, 232
telephone hot lines, 213
testing
    and father-daughter relation-
        ships, 109, 120
    and mother-daughter relation-
        ships, 8, 33, 42–43
therapy/therapists, 1, 2, 192, 204.
        See also type of therapy
tongue studs, example of, 43–48
traditional mothers archetype, 98
trust
    and commonly experienced
        emotional problems, 193
    and communication between
        mother and daughter, 88
    and father-daughter relation-
        ships, 104, 111, 113, 116,
        119
    and how and when to
        intervene, 184
    and issues facing daughters and
        mothers, 182
    and mother-daughter relation-
        ships, 48
    and sex/sexuality, 179
    and what daughters say about
        mothers, 228

values and standards, 56, 167, 212
vegetarianism, 152–153, 161, 219
verbal abuse, 8, 28

victimization, 211
violence, 181, 204–205, 210
vitamins, 151, 152, 221

wanting what is best, 56
weight
    and body image basics, 16, 20
    and communication between
        mother and daughter, 84
    and dating violence, 205
    and eating disorders, 199
    and food and nutrition, 142,
        154–155, 156
    of mothers, 16, 20, 220, 222,
        223, 224

and peer pressures, 156
resources about, 233
and what daughters say about
    mothers, 217, 218–223, 224,
    232
See also eating; fat; food
Weight Watchers, 155
Whatever Age, 73
The What's Happening to My Body?
    (Madaras), 23
withdrawal, and commonly
    experienced emotional
    problems, 194
Wolf, Naomi, 60–62
women, putting down, 127

ABOUT THE AUTHORS

STEPHANIE PIERSON has written books and magazine articles on teens, family, food, and lifestyle issues; she appeared on *The Oprah Winfrey Show*, *The View*, and the *Oxygen Network*. She is a creative director at a New York advertising agency and a contributing editor for *Metropolitan Home* magazine. She lives with her family in New York State.

PHYLLIS COHEN, C.S.W., is a clinical social worker and psychotherapist who has had a full-time private practice in Manhattan and Brooklyn for more than twenty-five years. She lectures on issues of adolescence and is a co-founder and former Clinical Director for the Brooklyn Center for Families in Crisis.

Buy Vermilion Books

Order further Vermilion titles from your local bookshop, or have them delivered direct to your door by Bookpost

☐ **Ophelia's Mum** by Nina Shandler   0091884152 £9.99

☐ **Anorexia and Bulimia**
    by Dr Dee Dawson   0091876524 £8.99

☐ **Overcoming Overeating**
    by Jane Hirschmann   009182561X £6.99

☐ **Helping Your Anxious Child**
    by Dr David Lewis   0091884330 £7.99

☐ **The Parents' Complete Guide**
    to Young People and Drugs
    by James Kay and Julian Cohen   0091815533 £8.99

☐ **The Model Plan** by Maryon Stewart 0091882427 £7.99

☐ **Sisters Unlimited** by Jessica Howie 0091884160 £12.99

FREE POST AND PACKING
Overseas customers allow £2.00 per paperback

ORDER:

By phone: 01624 677237

By post: Random House Books
c/o Bookpost
PO Box 29
Douglas
Isle of Man, IM99 1BQ

By fax: 01624 670923

By email: bookshop@enterprise.net

Cheques (payable to Bookpost) and credit cards accepted

Prices and availability subject to change without notice.
Allow 28 days for delivery.
When placing your order, please mention if you do not wish to receive
any additional information

www.randomhouse.co.uk